Off the Rocks

Volume 16

An Anthology of GLBT Writing

Published by NewTown Writers Chicago

Edited by Allison Fradkin

<2>

<3>

Cover art by Ira Joel Haber.

Now in our 32nd year, NewTown Writers Chicago is proud to publish, perform, and promote the work of GLBT writers. Created by Randy Gresham in 1980, NewTown Writers continues to uphold its commitment to the local, national, and international GLBT community, providing us with a multitude of opportunities to speak up and speak out, and to be heard loud and queer.

<5>

Table of Contents

7 < Introduction >

9 < What to Do When Your Best Friend's Diva Dies > Jarrett Neal

15 < Eliot on the Bayou > Robert Klein Engler

17 < I Stare (The Beauty of Boys and Girls) > Nicole Goodwin

19 < Transitions > Jason Orne

27 < To Moustaches > Megan Backer-Bertsch

31 < You're a Woman Now > Caitlin Hoffman

35 < Blades for a Mermaid's Grace > Elizabeth Barrette

37 < I Bequeath Myself > Scott Wiggerman

39 < The Shape of the Earth > Gary McCann

53 < The Airship > Adrian Ford

55 < Unus Mundi > Denise Roma

61 < Jason > Anders Krug Waalen

63 < Over Easy > Austin Eichelberger

69 < Granville > Tyler Gillespie

71 < You're So Skin Tight > B.M. Spaethe

73 < San Francisco > Barry Frauman

75 < Personal and Political > O.C. Devanney

85 < On Dating a Jewish Girl > Sarah Fonseca

87 < Forgiveness > Vince Sgambati

<6>

101 < Stranger > Martin Altman

103 < Pounce > Chelsey Clammer

113 < Generic Butch-Femme Poem > Andrea Lambert

115 < How to Start Being (Gay) > Timothy David Rey

117 < The Skeleton in My Closet > Ryan M. Mattern

119 < National Coming Out Day 2011 > Walter Beck

121 < Yesterdays and Tomorrows > H.L. Sudler

127 < First Aid > Daniel W.K. Lee

129 < Strength Starts the "It Gets Moderately More Tolerable"
Campaign > Marty McConnell

131 < For Tyler Clementi > Sarah Fonseca

133 < Livin' on a Prayer > Dario Dalla Lasta

139 < Thanking My Lucky Star > Allison Fradkin

143 < Ejaculating Beauty > Aimee Herman

161 < About the Contributors >

167 < About the Editor >

<7>

Introduction

How do you identify? Do you ident-defy? What are your identities? Do you identi-tease? Do you transpose, transgress, transcend? In putting together this year's edition of *Off the Rocks*, I noticed that many of the pieces endeavor to explore identity. This made me question how I identify: as a femme lesbian.

Femmes are not readily identifiable in the mainstream. Butch lesbians are still the most visible genre, if you will. Femme lesbians, on the other hand, are presumed straight until or unless proven otherwise. This invisibility, this anonymity, means that even though I am out as a femme, I am still in the closet as a lesbian.

On the bright side, because people cannot ascertain a femme's sexual identity with a cursory glance, we pose a threat to the status quo. Femmes are the dykes to watch out for. It's a simple case of queer and present danger.

This subversion of gender norms is perhaps the greatest reward of being a femme-identified lesbian. We have the power to challenge—and change—people's preconceived notions about women, about lesbians, about femininity. When I come out to others, they are compelled to question all of the deep-seated stereotypes about lesbians that they have internalized.

They are forced to face the realization that contrary to what they have been taught, a woman's attraction to the opposite sex is not the natural order of things.

They are obliged to concede that the categories of "woman," "feminine," and "heterosexual" are not nearly as interchangeable or inexorable as they have been led to believe.

They are forced to acknowledge that a feminine gender presentation and a lesbian sexual orientation are compatible. In other words, that heterosexuality is no more a requirement for womanhood than masculinity is a requirement for lesbianism.

They are forced to come to terms with the fact that lesbian relationships are multifarious and multifaceted;

<8>

that not all femmes couple with butches; and that femmes who partner with butches are not attempting to recreate heterosexual relationships or replicate male/female gender roles.

It has occurred to me throughout the process of deconstructing my femme identity that perhaps I should reconsider the identifying terms that I use. The imperative of classification, of the compartmentalization of identities, reveals the limitations of the femme label.

For one thing, the word implies its butch counterpart, inadvertently reinforcing the notion that there are two and only two kinds of lesbians, and that identifying as a lesbian necessitates entry into one category or the other. Such an obligation means that there is no room to move within, between, or outside of the dichotomy.

I propose reconfiguring femme and feminine as femmeinine, defined as the coherent fusion of a feminine gender presentation with a lesbian sexual orientation.

Being femmeinine is a self-affirming identity that transcends dress and deportment. It is not about appropriating (or misappropriating) the trappings of heterosexuality.

It is a way of signifying one's desire to defy and shatter stereotypes.

It is a way of rejecting and resisting homophobia, sexism, heterosexism, and compulsory heterosexuality.

It is a way of subverting gender norms that are designed to constrict women's self-expression, sexual subjectivity, and sexual object choice.

It is a way of facilitating the dissolution of the inequities and oppressive ideologies that have contributed to the stigmatization of lesbians.

Femmeininity is both transgressive and progressive: it translates anonymity into action, invisibility into initiative.

<9>

Jarrett Neal

What to Do When Your Best Friend's Diva Dies

Listen closely. Once you get all the details, turn off the television, then the oven. Take out the chicken breasts and place them in a plastic container. After you put the container in the refrigerator, call your best friend—do not text him—and ask him if he's okay. He'll be crying. Even if he laughs once or twice on the phone, even if he's trashing her last album or the ugly dress she wore to the Grammys last year, don't agree with him. He'll sob or screech at any derisive comments you make about her. Even if he says he's fine, drive to his apartment. Be patient.

If your diva is already dead, think about her briefly as you grab your car keys, leave your apartment, and walk to your car. Her songs will make you smile and you may begin to hum them. Imagine she's watching over you like a guardian angel, clichéd though it may be. She is your nostalgia; the remembrance of a bygone era of good feelings; a symbol as antiquated as red neckties, green carnations, and colored handkerchiefs. Yet you and others still adore her, still rely on her to be your beacon and your comforting embrace. Feel glad that you don't have to mourn your diva again. Get all thoughts of her out of your mind before you arrive at your best friend's place. Don't congratulate yourself. This is your best friend's sorrow, not your moment in the spotlight.

If his diva were your diva, too, cry at home by yourself before you leave. Weep. Sob. Blubber. Curse her husband, her ex-husband, her parents, her agents, and the entire entertainment industry for not coming to her rescue. Blame God, her fans, and critics. The catharsis you experience after you shed your last tear will leave you feeling so refreshed you'll wonder, for a fleeting moment, why you don't cry like this more often. After you've composed yourself, get in the car and play her songs on the stereo on the drive to your best friend's apartment. Turn

<10>

up the volume. You'll know the lyrics to at least a dozen of her songs already. Sing along. Remember her videos. Remember when you and your best friend went to her concert together and screamed like old ladies at a church revival filled with the Holy Spirit. Remember waving your arms, swinging your hips, and shaking your rumps to her club remixes.

Remember her appearances on *Oprah* and *Ellen*. Remember how the sound of her voice, the ear-splitting notes she hit, the personal demons she struggled to overcome—addiction, bad marriages, poor health, miscarriages, sexual abuse, or a combination of these—helped you, your best friend, and legions of fans learn to love yourselves, defy convention, summon the courage to come out of the closet, go back to school, mentor drug- addicted cousins, nurse an ailing parent, leave an abusive husband or boyfriend. At this point, hold back any tears you feel like shedding.

If his diva weren't your diva, if you hated her with a fury you reserve for Republicans and able-bodied people who park their cars in handicapped parking spaces, keep your snide comments to yourself. Don't mention the weight his diva put on, the cavalcade of men she slept with, the troop of adopted Third World children she carted around like designer luggage, the addiction she couldn't kick, the publicity stunts gone wrong, or the inane comments she made regarding politics. Praise all of her songs. Don't say she never had any talent. Don't say she was derivative. Don't say you knew all along that a woman like her would come to a tragic end.

Remember that she was human just like you and she tried her best to make the most of her life. Remember your own faults: the student loan debt you struggle to pay, the time you pushed your kid brother out of his wheelchair when you were nine-years-old, the year you spent whoring after you lost both your partner and your job within weeks, the evil looks you give old ladies who haggle over the price of fruit in grocery store check-out lines. Think of the dead diva's acts of charity, disingenuous though they may have been. Learn the lyrics to three of the dead diva's biggest

<11>

hits. This will be a true testament to your friendship, and your best friend will appreciate your solidarity. Remember, that's what it's all about—solidarity. Be kind.

Arrive at your best friend's apartment with a bag of his favorite junk food. Buy plenty of it. Hug him as tight as you can. His diva's music will be blasting on his stereo. News channels reporting his diva's death will be playing on his television. If she died of an overdose, he'll sob at regular intervals. If she died of natural causes, he may be done crying. Go home and reheat your chicken breasts if this is the case. If she died in a freak accident like an airplane or car crash, if she were gunned down by a deranged fan, or if she committed suicide, be prepared to stay all night.

Your best friend will want to go to the nearest gay bar to mourn with others. Take him even if it is a weeknight and you have to go to work the next day. When you arrive, the bar will be packed. Don't sigh or complain. Pay his cover. Buy all of his drinks. His diva's videos will be playing on every flatscreen. Half of the patrons will speak fondly of her. The other half will complain that they never could stand her and that her death is a blessing. If your best friend hears this and wants to start a fight, take him outside and walk around the block with him until he calms down. He'll cry a little. Wrap your arm around his shoulders. Call the guys in the bar a bunch of bitchy queens. He'll appreciate this more than anything else you've done so far.

Go back to the bar if he wants to. If he catches you yawning and asks if you'd like to go home, smile and tell him you're just fine. Buy another round of drinks. His diva's videos will still be playing on the flatscreens. Sing along with them, especially the songs he knows you hate. He'll appreciate this. He'll start to get tipsy at this point and rail about Prop 8, *Brokeback Mountain*'s loss, Matthew Shepard, and Westboro Baptist Church. Let him rant but don't buy him anymore drinks. If he starts to talk about his ex-boyfriend, persuade him to drink a glass of water. If he starts to cry over his diva again, relax—he's almost over his grief. If he starts to sob over the time his

<12>

father called him a dirty faggot, take him home as quickly as possible.

The sun will be coming up by the time you unlock his front door. He'll be too drunk to do it himself. If this is a weekend, go back home and stay in bed all day. If this is a weeknight, go home and drink a big cup of coffee. Shower, dress, go to work. Struggle through a miserable day and go right to sleep when you get home. In any event, stop thinking about yourself. This is your best friend's sorrow, not your moment in the spotlight.

He'll be singing his diva's songs when he stumbles into the apartment. Tell him to keep his voice down. If he's late paying rent, his landlord will be looking for any reason to evict him. If he owns a condo, the neighbors will gossip. His gait will be unsteady and he'll sound like John Wayne after a massive stroke. Tell him this. It will make both of you laugh. If he has to throw up, rush him to the bathroom and hold a cold, wet cloth on the back of his neck. He'll have a picture of his diva framed on the bathroom wall. It may be autographed; it may bear the diva's luscious scarlet lip print. Her expression will be regal, rarified, resolute. Compliment her picture even though your best friend probably won't remember what you said. Take him by the arm. He'll insist on rinsing his mouth with Scope. Let him. Don't judge.

Afterwards, take him to his bedroom. He'll collapse on his bed and try to take off his clothes. He'll be too drunk to do it, so you'll have to take his clothes off for him. Strip him down to his underwear. He'll make a dirty comment. Laugh heartily; it will make the situation feel less awkward. Ask him if he's going to be okay. He'll say yes.

Tell him how sorry you are that his diva died, but don't be surprised if he insults your diva. He's allowed. Don't look at your watch. Don't check your cellphone. Don't look at his languid, nearly naked body in the glow of sunrise. If he rises from the bed, presses his body to yours, and kisses you, let him, but don't move your lips. You'll be surprised, but you won't be shocked. Hug him after the kiss, not during the kiss—this above all else is crucial. If he tries to unzip your fly, make a joke, push his hands away, and leave

<13>

the apartment. If he laughs and asks why the two of you couldn't make things work years ago, smile and shrug. Say nothing. What the two of you have now is beyond words. Your best friend will pass out after this. Place a glass of water and two aspirin on his nightstand. If he has fresh fruit in his kitchen, like a banana or an apple, leave it on the nightstand, too. Don't slam the front door or the neighbors will get the wrong idea about him. Don't stand in the hall. Don't think about it, even though it won't go away. Don't despair.

<14>

Off the Rocks

Robert Klein Engler

Eliot on the Bayou

Look down on me, General Lee, from your leg of stone, see
me lookin' in the shop window at the simple, childhood joy
of usin' cotton for snow, while heavy keys dangle from da
hardware of Grandma's old purse and she takes one sore
step after another to market and remembers how dey sing
down here, "When love goes wrong, nothin' goes right," so
her days are a blur, dust assembles in the corners and on
the stairs, she's hungry, but weary of cooking, even the
ghosts at her table have no faces, and at the nearby bar a
video pounds and pounds out the heartbeat, "You are the
one, the one, the one," and all the men on the posters have
washboard abs, so she gives a glance and remembers,
bending over her washboard, up and down, slosh, slosh,
slosh, in and out of the gray water, it was so hard to get
blood out of cotton, damn, she wants a cigarette bad, and
then to watch TV with a stiff drink, while the smoke curls
into a shaft of light, almost as if it were writing in light with
gray light, like the ferns that grow out of a crack in the
mortar, between the bricks, up high, holdin' on best they
can, when a cold front comes in from Texas and turns the
sky above New Orleans azure blue with bright sunlight that
reflects off the wax magnolia leaves to change them from
hunter green to white, just like Dante wrote, and look, the
anger in the human heart may see where to go into despair,
and, General Lee, on your leg of stone, look down on me
and on the Big Easy dat oft times ain't so easy, where so
many wander like the pigeons over the palms, that wheel
and wheel above, unable to decide on a place to land and
learn the modern truth: less is simply less, even at the
gates to the beyond, where the guard demands, "Are you
bringing anything back?" and she say, "Just this body and
these bones. Just these dreams," den past the Creole
restaurant where the waiter spends his time talkin' to the
young couple in the corner of the room because her

<16>

husband's hot, and he's humpin' her, too, just the ordinary ups and downs, ins and outs, but with money to boot, 'cuz dem high-class boys got an air about demselves, and dey can wear pink and not bother about what it means or how love flutters as a candle flame, to make all flesh look better, then fluctuates and fades; honestly, all those birth pangs, yet dey hanged him all da same 'cuz his grandma stood in chains out on Algiers Point, den a white man caught her eye, oh, yeah, just the ordinary up and down, da bump and grind, da forward and behind dat makes some saints weep uncontrollably when they ponder the world of men, oh, yeah, da in and out, da up and down, General Lee, look down on us and the artist who got dem tits high and just right in the drawin' he burnt on glass with acid for da Sazerac Saloon, and look down on the poet who etches paper with the acid of words, he's not alone, he's got da ghost of a lover to conjure from da days when he was pure and refused to touch what he desired, General Lee, let the good times roll away from the days when he is old and no one will touch him, and let her buy somethin' at da A&P, bread maybe—don't have to cook dat—tuna, too, then back home where one bowl is on the table and a flame burns in the Jesus candle, and she could be saved by hope, don't ya hope so, for all our sake, too, 'cuz such is the choice between fire and, oops, more fire; like he say, you want dat boy, you want dat girl, caught in da bright mystique of our desire; there is for all one choice—pick fire or fire.

Off the Rocks

<17>

Nicole Goodwin

I Stare (The Beauty of Boys and Girls)

I

I stare at beautiful boys,
In all their wicked glow.

I chase them with my eyes
I steal them with my glance

And I absorb them into my skin
Tightly,
Never to let them go.

II

I stare at gorgeous girls
I notice them with my smile.

I climb into their hearts,
I steal their breath with a kiss.

I carry them away,
in the darkness
Of my chariot.

They absorb into my skin.
I never let them go.

III

When I finally accepted who I was
I began to understand.

When I had lost all of my shame
I forgot the meaning of guilt.

<18>

I embrace love, both masculine
And feminine

I take a bite into all that is good
Godly,
I sink my teeth inside another's body
I savor the taste of my own self.

<19>

Jason Orne

Transitions

"I'll take the cavatelli," I said to the waitress. I had just tried my hand at making the little flicks three days before. My index finger still hurt from the endless flicking of tiny pieces of pasta dough, cut from a long, thin noodle. I had pressed my finger into the middle of the little lump, and then rolled it back toward myself. The backward flick of my finger caused the dough to elongate, curling around itself until it had formed little tunnels. Well, at least some of them formed tunnels.

The cavatelli that arrived at my table in the restaurant, Underground Kitchen, only bore a vague resemblance to those that I had made over the wooden counter at home. Different dough, different technique. Made from spinach pasta, these ones were bright green. "These are two-finger cavatelli," I told my date, making inane conversation. He didn't seem to know quite how to respond.

Neither did I. Clearly, things go better when you know what you're getting yourself into.

Yet, even when you think you know what you're doing, you can still be surprised. Even with all my experience and preparation, things can turn out badly. You can still be surprised at yourself and your own reactions. Surprised at the difference between the way one thinks one will react and the way one's body and emotions respond to being in that moment. The difference between agreeing to go on a date and actually sitting down across from someone you realize you are not attracted to.

We met on OkCupid, an online dating Web site that attempts to match people based on user-submitted questions. Our score: 96%. Reading his profile did not take that long, considering that his responses were much shorter than the typical paragraphs full of subtle self-compliments—like my profile, for example. Despite the

<20>

tiny picture from the vague angle, I thought he looked cute enough to warrant a first date.

"Great profile! I like how you note that you're a queer, anti-racist feminist. Me, too! How are you doing?"

His responses were quirky, witty, and on-point. The kind of banter that I expect out of my dates. Of all of my previous boyfriends, only my ex-partner Andrew had been able to keep up. If I use the cliché "my words drip with sarcasm," it is only because I expect my partners to have put on their galoshes, raincoat, and open up an umbrella. Andrew had been able to trade barbs with the best of them.

After being together for four-and-a-half years, I had asked him to marry me. I flew out to California, where he was finishing up his graduate school program, and gave him a Tiffany platinum wedding band studded with diamonds on the beach of our favorite scuba diving reef. Pictures, phone calls, and status updates on Facebook followed. We drove 2,000 miles across the country to move together again.

Three months later in early November, it was over.

By March, I thought I was ready again to dip my toes in the local dating pool. OkCupid seemed an easy place to start dating again, mostly because unlike other dating sites, the gay men here didn't only want to come over to my house to have sex. It might have been a while since I'd been on dates, but I was ready to make the jump.

After a few more messages back and forth with my new date, we agreed to meet at Underground Kitchen the next night. It was the final message he sent me that started my own personal anxiety:

"See you tomorrow. I'll be wearing a blue checkered shirt. Also, FYI: I'm a transguy, just in case you were, like, expecting a dude or something. Talk to you tomorrow!"

Ostensibly, that was fine by me. I prefer the term "queer" to "gay," if only for my oft anti-assimilationist politics. I had just been teaching human sexuality the previous semester, telling my students that our categories of gender and sexuality were too limited to capture the full diversity of who people are and what they like to do with their bodies. I knew what a transguy was: FTM, trans-

<21>

gendered, someone who was born with a particular biological body that was assigned a female sex at birth but now identified with a male gender, or outside of those categories completely.

At least that was the reaction I knew I should be having. My trans-inclusive politics and beliefs chided me for my initial reaction to cancel. I already didn't do well on first dates, especially the first dates that I had been having lately. Having only been out of my relationship for a short time, just enough for me to convince myself that the only way to get over Andrew was to start putting someone else's spit in my mouth, I already routinely chickened out at the last minute on all but the most promising meetings. I was not OkCupid's star user.

Honestly, I was uncertain about which would be the more bigoted reaction: cancel because I learned that he was trans and was unsure if I would be able to be attracted to his biological female body or keep the date when I was aware of this possibility, partially to convince myself that I am the type of person that would go on a date with a transperson.

Furthermore, I was, and am still, unsure about what it would mean for my own sexuality if I arrived at the restaurant and was blown away by his handsomeness. If one's sex is biological and one's gender is cultural, which is a gay man attracted to? Is it possible for me to separate those myself?

While I wouldn't describe myself as 100% gay, any lesser percentage was entirely theoretical. I knew that I wanted to only be involved romantically and emotionally with men. I had kissed women before, usually while I was drunk, but I just wasn't interested in going further. In the time leading up to the date, I felt increasingly anxious. I knew I would be attracted to his masculinity, but would I even be able to get an erection for his biobody? Shouldn't I respect the gender he identifies as, untainted by the biological sex he was born with?

This is a set of sexual identity transitions that I had witnessed several of my close lesbian friends go through while I was in college, but I did not know of any gay male

<22>

friends who had gone through similar situations. Sarah, a friend who helped me run a queer political group, told me drunkenly one night, each of us holding a red plastic college cupful of a knockout potion called Trashcan Punch, that she was unsure whether she should call herself a lesbian now that she had fallen in love with a transman.

He identified as a man and lesbians didn't date men. That seemed to be the gist of it in her eyes. Her confusion lay in that she did not find any other men attractive nor did she want to have any kind of heterosexual sex. "I don't find dicks attractive. I like his cunt," she confessed. That didn't appear to be a problem, since her boyfriend didn't plan to get bottom surgery, but Sarah's identity was still shaken by the prospect.

Sarah is not the only lesbian I know to find herself destabilized by a partner's transition. The traditional butch/femme dynamic, while waning today in its oppressive necessity within lesbian communities, originally provided a space for gender non-conforming masculine-identified women to escape solely feminine relationship roles. With the rise of trans-activism and the increasing availability of transgender identities, the '80s and '90s saw an explosion in transitioning within lesbian communities. Even today, it's much more common for trans and gender-queer people to be involved in a lesbian social circle.

There doesn't seem to be a similar space for transpeople within gay male spaces. While I probably couldn't count the number of transguy/woman couples that I know, I don't personally know of a single gay biomale/gay transman pairing, although of course those pairings do happen. Sure, a psychologist would probably throw research at me about the supposed greater sexual identity flexibility of women, but I think it's something else. Part of masculine gay sexuality in America seems to be the repudiation of femininity, distance from women, and disgust with the female body.

It's almost assumed that gay men are disgusted by vaginas, as if it's part of a gay man's identity to be thoroughly grossed out by women's bodies. Gay men who have never been "subjected" to the horrors of the vagina

<23>

are called Gold Star Gays. Once, in the '90s, Dan Savage, the gay sex advice columnist, compared the female anatomy to a canned ham dropped from a great height. Even my own friends, despite knowing about my feminism, are convinced that I am going to be disgusted by any contact with a woman. When I played spin-the-bottle in college and a woman spun and it landed pointing at me, everyone would laugh and spin it again.

Yet how much of it is a choice? Is this a conscious rejection of women, who are often the vocal supporters and best friends, fruit flies, and fag hags in gay men's lives? I don't think so.

I know that because my body betrayed me.

When I saw my date the next day, reading a book at one of the silver, metal patio tables of the restaurant, even from far away I knew he didn't pass—that is, that his gender presentation was androgynously queer, rather than undetectably masculine. I waved as I approached and we shook hands. Andrew.

As if I didn't have enough Andrews in my life. The name reminded me of how new at this I was.

Andrew's black hat had a small red star in the corner, covering what he would later reveal as a short, stylish fauxhawk. Sure enough, he had on a blue checkered shirt, the pattern reminding me of a tablecloth or of the kind of curtains that I had seen in French bed and breakfasts. Blue denim and thick brown boots completed the ensemble.

It was the feminine curves of his face that I noticed at once. His smooth face, soft hands, and voice became evident shortly afterwards. I couldn't stop myself from prematurely getting into his business. Inappropriate thoughts like: *Had he already started taking T?, Did he plan to physically transition?, Was he binding right now?* flitted through my head. But I wasn't stupid enough to say them out loud.

I'm not sure I would have been looking had he not outed his transness to me before our date. It was as though I was looking for the various signs of female bodied-ness, judging his gendered worthiness to date. By my own metrics, I'm not sure my ex or I would pass my ultra-

<24>

masculine gender test. Andrew's, my Ex-Andrew's, oval curved face probably hadn't seen a razor in years. I've been told that I actually look quite masculinely conservative... until I open my mouth. Transcribing my own interviews for my Master's thesis was torture because I could barely recognize my own faggy voice.

I couldn't be a bigot, though, I thought—I mean, at least I was going on the date.

Then again, those are the kinds of things that people say when they are caught with their unknown prejudices and privilege: I have lots of black friends! But I love Korean food! My best friend is gay!

Did it make it any better just because it was my body that wasn't fitting my politics?

The personal is political, they say. I had just forgotten that therefore, even my dick was political. It may not have felt like a reaction that was under my control, but that didn't make it any less a rejection based on my own prejudices and social programming.

Throughout the dinner, I was distracted and, I must admit, probably not the best date. Although usually reported to be quite witty, my preoccupation with myself, my identity, my politics, and what did this mean, left me talking about the pasta rather than trying to honestly evaluate our compatibility. Describing the steps to produce cavatelli, I succumbed to babbling to cover my own discomfort with my reactions.

Later regaling Ex-Andrew with this chain of events, he reacted: "So what?" Who cares if I wasn't attracted to him? How was this any different than if I showed up to any other date and wasn't attracted to the other person? Does it make me transphobic just because I'm not attracted to this particular transperson? Isn't it even more transphobic to make a broad generalization about trans-people based on the one date with this one transguy?

I remain torn, because isn't this the same excuse that many people give Ex-Andrew about his Asian-American-ness? "I'm just not attracted to Asians," they'll say. "People are allowed to not be attracted to someone. It's just my preference." People feel attraction as a natural bodily

<25>

reaction. I did that day sitting down to eat. Yet, just because it felt natural doesn't mean that it wasn't shaped by our society's prejudices and oppressions, whether on the basis of race or gender.

Sitting down to eat pasta with Andrew sparked transitions of my own, a load of feelings, and a breakdown in the binary of straight-gay and male-female. I thought I would be so prepared—Queer Studies major in college and teaching human sexuality classes—but instead the result was mediocre. What did it mean for my sexuality? What was gender and what was masculine enough? Was I ready to start dating again after so long off the wagon? This date felt like a momentous occasion, full of anxiety and decisions.

But all Andrew wanted was to go on a date. How is that fair?

<26>

Off the Rocks

<27>

Megan Backer-Bertsch

To Moustaches

What I wouldn't do for my very own
moustache. My brother, thin-haired
and brittle, just grew one
for the hell of it, shaved it off
like an afterthought. I wish I could

have peeled it off his face, stolen
his eyes for the irony. I've been counting
them around the city for years, by far
my favorite being the Saint Patrick's Day
moustache, dyed green, rolled in wax,

maybe sculpted in a snood, and gently
dipped in frothy ale, the odorous
remnants of corned beef wafting at
his mate in the early afternoon
as he stumbles home from Parade

Day. My father has what is called a classic
Chevron, most notably found on athletes
in the '80s and '90s, but always trusty
on my dad. Once, when he shaved it off,
I didn't trust him because my mother

always said don't trust a man
with a thin upper lip. I pulled on it
as a kid and tried to find its magical
follicle source, the dark tubes
coming through like my Play-Doh Spaghetti

Factory Playset. I heard they renamed
the entire month of November "Mo-
vember," and for 30 days, men don't shave
their maw and it's all to fight testicular

<28>

cancer and I wonder what do women grow

for breast cancer and I wonder how
to grow my own testicles. Some men can
grow one thing but not the other but between
a moustache, a beard, or chest hair,
I'd still pick a 'stache even though

the hairiest man I've ever seen naked,
Burt Reynolds, made me feel less gay. Think
about it—the bristly awareness
of my own funk, like having my pubic
hair under my nose at all times to remind me

of the last time I fucked, or I ate, a scent
trail to map out my days. Like the last time
a pretty girl kissed me and left me minty
with her chapstick. I could squish
my lips up to my moustache and kiss her

all over again. Now think about the famous
moustaches in history: do we remember Hitler,
the man, or do we remember that swastika
under his lip, the same toothbrush
worn by Chaplin. Now are we laughing

still? And did Nietzsche talk to God
or did that bush do all the talking? When Dali
painted, did he utilize those vertical
tips to paint the drippy clocks
and elephants? Let the hipsters wax poetic

and the T-boys grow pubescent. No matter
what age they are, it's never too late
to cultivate a boyhood or a hair or two
on my own face, compared to the 10,000
on your average gentleman. Hey, I'll take 'em

but, you know, I've actually paid
to have a black wax moustache

<29>

smothered on my face just to have it
ripped right off for 15 bucks a pop,
my mighty pelt thrown away. We've been told

if we keep growing, there's a sideshow
with our names up on the marquee. But
when I'm old I'll grow it out with my hair
and India would have nothing
on me. Me and Frida will be

just a couple of old men in rocking chairs
twiddling our handlebars, and we're singing
the blues because the only king
in the whole deck without a moustache
is the King of Hearts.

Off the Rocks

<30>

<31>

Caitlin Hoffman

You're a Woman Now

Mother combs my hair, kissing it as she tucks violets into the knots. Her tears wet my neck; they are tears of joy, elation, relief. They are tears I do not share.

"I'm so proud of you," she says. "My little girl..."

Grabbing at her hand, I silence her with a smile. "Yes, Mother."

She puts kisses on my fingernails, upsetting the polish that has not yet dried. Then she guides me toward the vanity, so I can take a look at myself. My reflection awaits me.

The person staring back at me is not at all familiar. Stained lips, thick eyelashes, and tender skin without a crack or bruise, without any natural indication of the burning soul so far underneath. I burn, I drown, I bleed. Still, my face remains picturesque, intact, even luminescent. The make-up nicely covers the anxiety and stress.

The powder will not flake. It will not surrender to the truth.

I will remain concealed.

Still stripped to my undergarments, I have my stockings around my ankles and my bustier untied. Whilst my mother constricts my curves and connects garter belt to garters and garters to pantyhose, I am ultimately absent. My smile is strained, my laughter pressed between my teeth. I smile for my mother and for the rest of the world, but it is a smile that does not transfer internally.

"Now," my mother begins, and her voice is small, "it's best I tell you of your duty as a wife."

Absently, my fingers trail against the hem of my dress, pulled over my arms and onto my shoulders. When my head pops out again, I swallow. There is a lump in my throat that will not dissolve. It hinders my speech, but evidently, words are not necessary.

Off the Rocks

<32>

My mother continues speaking all the same, in no need of a reply. "You know what will be expected of you. You will take care of the house, make his dinners, and you will also be expected to bear him children."

My hand touches my stomach, lost beneath so many layers of lace. "Yes, Mother."

"On your wedding night..." Whatever it is she has to tell me causes a break in her voice. "Lie down, close your eyes. Just breathe. Let him..."

She cannot finish what must be said, and I don't press her. The truth is I don't want to know. I would like such things to remain ignored until I am forced to accept them.

Gently, she spins me around to face her. Now her eyes are filled with tears of a different kind. She touches my nose to hers, smiling through the pain. "My little girl. All grown up. Now, look what a pretty bride you make!"

Again, that stranger in the mirror stares at me. She intently scrutinizes me as I do the same to her. We desperately attempt to make contact, to recall where it was we've met before, but the connection is lost. I see no prettiness that my mother speaks of. In that stranger's eyes, I see only sadness. A restrained sadness, suffocated by make-up and the veil against my cheek.

I close my eyes and try to breathe. Mother rubs my shoulders to facilitate the process, but oxygen will not come. As it is, oxygen doesn't seem to matter.

Even airless, I am still beautiful.

Breathless, I will make the perfect wife.

The strings, the grass, the arch above me. I see it all, hear the music march me forward, feel the cold cling of my father as he leads me to my destiny. Down at the end of the aisle is the man I'm going to marry. A handsome man, one I've never met before. A man with his fists clenched at either side, a man with a ferocious fire in his eyes. Eyes that make me want to run the other way. What sort of man would want to marry a woman he's never met?

I do as my mother advised: "Say nothing. Just smile."

My husband-to-be returns the smile, bowing his head slightly. His eyes flicker, revealing a darkness underneath.

Off the Rocks

<33>

I wonder what this married life has in store for me. I worry what might happen if I cannot live up to my husband's expectations.

Ankles shake. Eyelashes burst into seizure. Nobody notices these spastic, honest flaws. My make-up and dress are doing their work, and doing it well. Nobody can see the feelings underneath. They see only the gloves, the elegant curve of my body, the fabric down far, far past my knees. I am a princess of layers. The veil covers the make-up, and the make-up hides any remaining emotional blemish. In that moment, I am immortalized as a singular glimpse of perfection.

I am everything a woman should be.

Knees together, I stand in front of my betrothed. The preacher starts to speak, but I have run away again. I have retreated to a far corner of my mind that law or reason cannot touch. Against my will, my gaze is wandering, and it lands on a particular face in the smiling crowd. I see a girl about my age, with a bob of blond hair and a neck like a swan.

Her eyes scream at me. They dilate at my impending union. They make smoke against the bright-lit sky.

She is not smiling, but shaking. Others may mistake her tears as products of bliss for the happy couple before her. Perhaps they think she's jealous, wishing for a husband of her own.

True, envy dictates her actions, but it is an envy of another kind.

Everyone else accepts my façade, but she slices it asunder. With one look, she weakens all my resolve. I cannot hide from her. My pearly teeth and painted cheeks do not obscure the truth. Not when her gorgeous eyes are on me.

Her lips tremble. Lips I loved to kiss, lips that made me shudder with every gasp of my lungs.

Looking at them now, I experience the most brutal, honest revelation.

She is everything I want, and everything I will never have. After all, how could a woman have another woman? What sort of irregularity would that be? What sort of wrath

<34>

from God would that incur? Surely, love can only be found within constraints of the law.

It is as my mother always said: I am fated to be a wife. That is the natural way of things.

I will stay silent, smile bright, and complete every one of my womanly duties. I will bear my husband's children, and I will do as he asks when we lie down together at night. I will do his dishes and press his shirts. I will be the perfect wife.

And even as I cry, my make-up will never run.

<35>

Elizabeth Barrette

Blades for a Mermaid's Grace

She beaches herself on the stone of my heart,
wondering why her song cannot set its hook in me.
Her pearl necklace dries in the salt breeze;
her skin, too, sheds the white powder of brine.
The magic shell in her hand has the power
to split flesh from bone and cleave her sleek tail
into two naked legs. The stories of my childhood
whisper to me that her pain will be like walking
on red-hot knives, but I cannot stop her.
I have not the words to tell her that my body
quickens only to the touch of other men.
She will carve, and curve, and change, and
forever after her only grace will be that of death.
I have not the words to tell her not to do this thing,
not to present herself as other than what she truly is—
for I, too, have hidden myself behind false graces.
I, too, know the pain of dancing on knife-sharp lies.

<36>

<37>

Scott Wiggerman

I Bequeath Myself

for Bruce Noll

I was touched by Walt Whitman today.
His hands, cool as spring rain, cupped
the back of my neck, drew me
toward his chest, salt-and-pepper hairs
sputtering like live wires through the vee

of a spacious muslin shirt, aromatic
with the scent of workingman, sailor,
criminal, friend of the calamus.
I was touched by the shiny musket balls
of his eyes, their cocky come-on,

the confidence that bore down, invited
me to abandon convention, assured me that
the world was there for the tasting.
The plump lips emerged from a nest
of beard, forming words I'd heard

and read a hundred times before, but these
were hooks, baiting with promise,
luring me, creating a hunger for the blades
of grass lounging on his tongue,
clumped inside the pockets of his pants,

sprouting through the buttonholes of his fly
like wild green pubic hairs. I was touched
by Walt Whitman, his earthy desire—
slugs and worms and life teeming through
the soil between his toes, and I liked it.

<38>

Off the Rocks

<39>

Gary McCann

The Shape of the Earth

Pixie-sized Robert spots us across the living room. His vibrant gray eyes smile from baby-soft, mottled skin as he makes his way around and between his chatting guests. "Hello, boys. Fashionably late, I see." His voice playful, raspy, his hands dart out from the sleeves of a baggy maroon cardigan to land on our forearms. He offers a cheek to be kissed. A thick brown shock of hair swings out from Dave's forehead as he leans to oblige Robert.

I glance to see who I know among the middle-aged academics, the group nearest us moaning about four more years of Reagan, whose second inauguration was Tuesday. I'm startled to spot Ian in a circle of grad students across the room. On his arm is a willowy brunette with hair down to the small of her back; I've seen her drop him off at the bookstore recently.

I turn away, but Ian's blue-black head and long-sleeved red T-shirt glow in my peripheral vision. "What's the matter?" Dave asks.

"Nothing." I kiss Robert's cheek.

"I'll put the beer we brought in the kitchen," Dave says, and heads off.

After Robert and I exchange a few pleasantries, I lean down to his ear. "You know Ian Ryan?"

Robert laughs and plays at making insinuating eyes. "Melinda, my research assistant, brought him. She has excellent taste, don't you think?"

"She does. Ian works for me."

Robert flicks silver eyebrows. "Small world. Lucky you."

Ian sees me and looks as surprised as I was to see him. He turns his back and slips his arm around Melinda's waist. Her sleeveless mint dress looks suitable for a wedding, as though this casual party means more to her than it should; I like her for the needy life that suggests. In

<40>

my fantasy world, where Ian and I do wild things to each other's bodies, I'm willing to share him.

I figure when Dave returns from the kitchen, I'll introduce him to Ian and get my nervous moment over. I hired Ian at the bookstore four months ago and I've barely mentioned him at home, something Dave is bound to point out when he gets an eyeful of Ian's dark, Irish good looks.

Robert pats my forearm and excuses himself to say good night to a couple leaving. I turn and see Dave standing by the long dining table, talking to our friend Sandy, so I head toward them.

"Hi, sweetie!" I shout over "What's Love Got to Do with It?" as someone cranks up the volume in the family room. Sandy and I peck on the lips. "You're looking good," I tell her. She's short and always fighting weight.

"I'm going to put this in the refrigerator." Dave raises the six-pack to indicate it.

Sandy's red hair is stylishly boyish and frames a pretty face with a clear complexion. As I bend down to listen to her, my back toward the living room, Melinda passes from behind me, leading Ian by the hand. They stop at the far end of the table. While Melinda greets two women grad students, Ian picks up a vodka bottle and fills a tumbler more than halfway. I wink when he looks up. He nods hello, just barely, and pours orange juice into his vodka.

Sandy tugs my hand while I'm staring at Ian. "Let's go out back so I can smoke."

She leads me through the family room, between dancing couples who look tired on Friday night, too settled in life for partying hard, too love-handled. Outside, through a sliding glass door, the smokers are spilling from the patio onto the small lawn, made even smaller by dripping bamboo towering on three sides. Sandy and I stop near a round stone table damp from fog at the edge of light cast by the house.

A joint comes our way, and I decide one hit won't hurt. Holding smoke in my lungs, I stare through the glass door as Melinda and Ian join the dancers in the family room.

"You know Ian Ryan?" Sandy asks, following my eye.

I let out my smoke. "He works for me."

Off the Rocks

"He works for you?"

"You must know him, too?"

Ian's doing an M.A. in comp lit, and Sandy is Robert's secretary in the English department.

"I know Melinda better."

"You don't like her?"

"She's all right—a little headstrong." Frowning, Sandy draws on her cigarette and exhales through small nostrils. "I wouldn't do Ian any favors, babe."

"What have you got against Ian? I like him."

Sandy twists her mouth. "Speaking of people I don't like, how's Jane?"

"Away on a cruise, hallelujah." Jane owns Royal Books, the store I manage despite Jane's micromanaging. Sandy used to work for me, and Jane loved to hate her.

"You're a patient man," Sandy says. "I owe you big time for hooking me up with Robert—he's a dream of a boss."

"I figured he would be. So why don't you like Ian?"

Sandy shakes her head. The joint reappears and I let it pass.

Sandy stubs out her cigarette in a wet ashtray on the stone table, glances around at the other smokers, and crosses her arms with a shiver. We're both wearing sweaters and jeans. I slip my arm around her shoulders. "You're cold, sweetie. Let's go dance."

In the family room I maneuver us in among the crowd bumping and grinding to Blondie's "Rapture." Ian and Melinda are near us. Sandy looks more distressed than happy. She needs a boyfriend, I figure—a son in college and an ex-husband aren't enough. I reach out and brush my fingertips along her cheeks, and she brightens.

Robert joins us as "Rapture" blends into "My Baby Takes the Morning Train." I pull my gray sweater over my head and toss it among shed layers on a couch shoved against a wall. Robert's smiling eyes flit to my sleeveless white undershirt, and I grin. Drunk, Robert once told me that he likes 30-year-old blondes; I happen to be a 30-year-old blonde, the only one he knows, to my knowledge.

<42>

"I'm not into dancing tonight, boys!" Sandy shouts, and scoots away after air-kissing Robert and me.

As "Flashdance" begins, I'm facing Ian and Robert both, with Melinda to my side, also facing Ian and Robert. Judging by Ian's glazed-over eyes, I figure he chugged all the vodka he poured. On the lyric "what a feeling," he raises his arms, and I mentally trace the contours of his compact torso as his shirt rides above a navel that looks like an etching.

"Dance with Lenny, you two!" Robert shouts to Melinda. "People are leaving and I want to say good night."

I turn halfway toward Melinda. She smiles until Robert disappears, then gives me a look that says she knows I'm admiring her date and doesn't appreciate it. Fair enough, I think. "I need a beer."

Slipping between the dancers, I find my sweater on the couch and toss it over my shoulder. I wonder where Dave is.

He's not in the living room. From the hallway, I glance into Robert's den and see Dave sitting forward on a black leather sofa, his back to me, his large hands raised in a shrugging gesture. He's talking to an engineering professor named Brian, a young Paul Newman; Dave's in the biology department but knows Brian from playing city league baseball. Brian's pregnant wife, a lawyer, is with them.

I watch my partner sitting erect in a white pullover sweater, his long back straight, his face angular and, glimpsed from the side as he turns his head, relaxed and smiling, unselfconscious as usual. He doesn't know I'm watching him and thinking I made a good decision when I moved to California to be with him. I played around a little after I got here, before anyone had heard of AIDS, a bullet I dodged. I'm only the second man Dave's had sex with in his life. If in the beginning I asked myself whether I was in love with him, I didn't ask myself for long.

I glance at Brian and wonder if Dave's attracted to him. I'm sure Dave gets a hard-on for as many men as I do. He won't admit it—he's afraid of encouraging me. He thinks I don't have his willpower.

<43>

I turn and head for the kitchen, a pale, olive room with dark cabinets and a butcher block island laden with booze, soft drinks, and barely touched platters of broccoli and cheese, all glistening and looking artificial under a ceiling spotlight. I see bottles of Moosehead beer in melting ice in a cooler on the floor. After helping myself, I lean back against the counter and savor being alone in relative quiet.

Ian appears in the doorway, stops when he sees me, then takes a few unsteady steps to the island, where he picks up a Pepsi. I grin, watching him. "Did you down all the vodka you poured, Ian?"

Without answering, he faces me and leans against the stove. His tanned, square-tipped fingers fumble with the can till it snaps open and mist rises.

"Where's the lady you're with?" I ask.

"In the head." He raises the Pepsi to his mouth, and his Adam's apple bobs as he gulps. Lowering the can, he flexes its thin metal. "You should tell Mai-Ly you're giving me Jack's hours."

Yesterday Ian started bugging me about Jack's hours. Jack's quitting his five evenings, and Mai-Ly asked for them; I said fine. Then Ian asked if he could have them.

"You're drunk, Ian. Why do you want Jack's hours so bad?"

"So you and I won't be working at the same time."

"What? Like I'm the first man you've ever been attracted to?"

"You don't know what you're talking about, Lenny."

Melinda walks into the kitchen, and I take a swallow of my Moosehead. "Your date's had too much to drink."

"Oh, yes." Melinda shakes her head, tch-tching, and slips an arm around Ian's waist to steer him from the room.

I finish my beer in no hurry and toss the bottle into the trash under the sink.

Dave is still sitting on the leather couch in the den, angled toward Brian in an Eames chair. Brian's wife isn't with them. They're talking about the 49ers beating the Dolphins in the Super Bowl last Sunday; I couldn't care less.

Off the Rocks

<44>

Dave glances over as I sit down beside him. He looks back at Brian and keeps talking, but holds a hand my way. I take it, lean back, and map the bones in my cowboy's fingers while his relaxed voice takes turns with Brian's.

Yawning, Dave asks if I'm ready to go.

"Whenever you are."

"I should find my wife," Brian says, rising from his chair. We follow him out of the den.

Melinda and Ian are sitting on the living room sofa, Melinda talking to one of the grad students she greeted earlier. Ian's slouched down on the cushions, an ankle across his knee, his head tipped back against the top of the couch. He catches sight of Dave and me, and without lifting his head, rotates it to follow us as we pass. I look over my shoulder from the front door and meet his fixed blue eyes.

Saturday afternoon Ian and I are straining under the weight of a display table we're unloading from a U-Haul van in Jane's driveway, high in the hills above downtown Fullerton. Ian is housesitting for Jane while she cruises the Caribbean with her lawyer son and his wife. Her son is my age. Jane loves to tell me about the rich and successful things he's doing. I could be doing rich and successful things, too, if I'd inherited a small fortune from my grandparents.

Ian and I upend the display table against the wall in her chilly garage. I wipe my face with the front of my sweat-shirt. "We'll never use this goddamn table in the store again, but Jane can't throw anything away."

Ian shrugs at my irritation. I follow him out to the sunny driveway, and he lowers the garage door, hiding Jane's pink Cadillac. Her Spanish-style house sits above and to the side of the garage, on the highest point of a ridge. Newer houses—elegant ranchers—line the road as it descends in both directions from Jane's property.

Ian looks up cement steps curving to her front door through terraces shored up with wire mesh and planted with ivy and squat junipers. "Have you ever been inside?"

Off the Rocks

<45>

I shake my head. "I've heard enough about it—she has a nervous breakdown picking new shelf paper for the kitchen cabinets."

"The view's fantastic from the back. Do you want to see?"

"All right."

I follow him up the steps and in the front door. He leads me past a beige living room, with a wagon wheel coffee table, and out French doors to a patio. Santa Ana winds have blown away last night's fog, and the view at our feet encompasses much of North Orange County as it slopes toward the ocean.

Ian glances to see if I'm impressed. I refuse to be effusive over anything connected to Jane.

He points at what appears to be a low, brown cloud on the silver horizon. "That's Catalina."

I realize he's right. "I can see why you like staying here."

"At night, with the lights spread out below, it feels like you're in an airplane."

I watch his eye follow a jet, far enough away to look toy-like as it descends toward Orange County airport.

"I've only flown once in my life," he mumbles.

"Coming from Ireland?"

"Going to San Francisco. Well, twice—going and coming back. I've never been out of California except as a baby."

"When did you go to San Francisco?"

"A couple of years ago. This girl I knew took me for my birthday. All she wanted to do was stay in our hotel room and have sex."

I laugh out loud. "Were you a disappointment to her, Ian?"

"I wanted to go out and at least see *something*."

Smiling, I glance down a sheer embankment, blazing yellow with trailing gazanias. A rectangular swimming pool nestles on a cut in the chaparral-covered hillside, silver green from recent rain. The pale blue body of water is framed by dark blue tile. Weathered redwood lounges with faded green cushions stretch like lizards at odd angles to one another.

Ian follows my gaze to the pool. "Do you want to go for a swim? It's heated."

I stare at a steep flight of railroad-tie steps sunk into the cliff, with a round, rusty metal handrail on one side. The tops of eucalyptus trees mask the roofs of houses along a road a few hundred feet from the pool. "Sure, let's go for a swim."

As we strip off our clothes at the bottom of the steps, I watch the boom of a grasshopper oil derrick, around the curve of the hillside, rise and fall above ragged olive trees. Ian's light tan body shows a bathing suit line fainter than mine. I take a mental snapshot of his backside as he dives into the water, and then follow him. The pool is so full that ripples slosh onto the deck.

We swim laps, leisurely at first. When he swims faster, I stay with him.

He quits and glides to the side, turns to face inward and watch me. I swim several more laps before pulling up next to him. He's hugging the pool wall, his chest flush to it, gleaming arms folded in the sun on the dark blue tile edge, one hand over the other. I grip the lip and let my upright body sink lower in the water than his. The pool undulates from our swimming, and my chest drifts toward the wall and away as ripples nip the side.

"How'd you feel this morning, Ian, after all the vodka you drank last night?"

He doesn't answer. He lifts his arms off the tile edge and drops underwater to his chin.

"Do you remember coming into the kitchen for a Pepsi and talking to me?" I ask.

We're shoulder-to-shoulder. The wind is chilly on my head, and my nose is running and stinging from chlorine, all I can smell. I feel his toes caress the sole of my foot. He stretches toward me, and we kiss.

"Hello! *Hello*!" a voice shouts from above. "I'm *here*!"

We look up at Melinda.

"I'll be right there!" Ian bellows, his voice deep.

I stare at the top of the yellow-flowering embankment; Melinda is looking down over the patio railing.

Off the Rocks

<47>

Ian hoists himself out of the water. Melinda's not in sight when I look up again, before climbing onto the deck myself. Ian and I shiver in the wind. He kicks into his jeans, grabs his T-shirt, sweater, socks and shoes, and hustles up the railroad-tie steps.

Letting the air dry me some, I gaze around the hillside in the low sun's gold light. A jackrabbit emerges from the brush, and it and I watch each other as I pull on my pants and sweatshirt. It scampers away, and I pick up my old deck shoes and leisurely climb barefoot up the steps.

Melinda's in the kitchen. Her pink sweater, black jeans, and white tennis shoes remind me of a three-tone car from the fifties. Her hair is pulled back in a knot, her face bare except for pink lipstick. The smell of coffee fills the room, and the sound of a shower running comes from elsewhere in the house. Melinda lifts a pot from a coffeemaker. "Do you want some? You must be freezing."

"Thanks."

She fills a large white mug. Behind her, a curtain billows at one side of the window over the sink.

"Milk or sugar?"

"Black, please."

I take the mug and sit at the kitchen table, a battered antique of Shaker simplicity. Melinda picks up another white mug from the counter. Her light blue eyes watch me as though I'm an experimental mouse about to exhibit an important reaction. I swallow a little coffee.

She raises her eyebrows. The sound of the shower stops, and she glances toward the other room, then sips from her mug. She lowers it and pinches the bridge of her nose. "You wouldn't be here if..."

"I'm not your rival, Melinda."

"I'm not *your* rival."

"I'm in a relationship."

"Are you?"

A fat gray cat walks into the room, sits down, and wraps its tail around its rump. I've never seen Prudence before but feel like I know her from everything Jane's told me about her.

<48>

"Ian and I are friends," Melinda says. "I care what happens to him."

She and I stare at the cat until Ian pads into the room in shorts and a black T-shirt, his head wet. I gulp the last of my coffee, wiggle my feet into my deck shoes, and rise from my chair. "Time for me to go. See you at work, Ian."

He follows me toward the front of the house. I let myself out and hustle down the curving steps through the reinforced terraces. My beige Rabbit is parked beside the U-Haul van that Ian and I rented on Royal Books' credit card. I pat my steering wheel as I start the engine. I'm nervous backing up to make a three-point turn in Jane's driveway. Melinda arrived just in time, I realize. Dave and I have been monogamous since we put on wedding rings five years ago—I wasn't sure I could do it, but I have.

I plan to keep plenty of distance between me and Ian from now on.

I'm at Target the next day, buying underwear for Dave and me. He spends Sunday afternoons working in his office, on campus. He won't be back at the house till suppertime.

It's dark outdoors when my Rabbit bumps up the driveway of a Dunkin' Donuts shop near Cal State. I want a cup of coffee. I pull into a parking space facing the plate glass of the barebones eating room. As I shut off my engine, I glance through the lighted windows. Dave is sitting in one of the pastel Formica booths in the bright neon glare. He's leaning forward and grinning, holding a crumpled paper coffee cup, crushing the cup with his fingertips. Sitting across from Dave is Ian, also leaning forward and grinning, holding a bent drinking straw, wrapping the straw around his index finger.

I watch them. They look at the tabletop and look at each other.

They rise from the booth, and I start my car. They walk toward the door, laughing and talking, and I back out from my parking space. I roll quickly toward the driveway and out.

Off the Rocks

<49>

At home I pour a glass of red wine and take chicken breasts from the refrigerator, coat the breasts in olive oil, and season them for the grill. I take lettuce and tomatoes out of the crisper.

What could be keeping Dave? He and Ian ran into each other on campus, recognized each other from Robert's party, and went for a cup of coffee. Simple, I've decided.

The sound of his car idling in the alley behind our house tells me Dave's raising the garage door. I take broccoli out of the refrigerator, pare off the stems, and drop the florets into a steamer.

The kitchen door opens, and Dave comes in carrying his briefcase. After kissing me, he looks at the chicken on the counter. "Good. I'm hungry."

"I'll start the grill and we can eat early. How was your afternoon?"

"Okay."

He carries his briefcase into his den and goes into our bedroom, then returns to the kitchen with his sweater, shoes, and socks off, his white T-shirt covered with blue fuzz.

"Did you get a lot of work done?" I ask.

"Finished a draft of my article. Looked up some stuff in the library. What'd you do this afternoon?"

"Read. Went to buy underwear. I'm making coffee. Do you want a cup?"

"I had coffee just before I left the office. Should I throw together the salad?"

"If you want to. Maybe I won't bother making coffee."

A small red ant crawls across the faded kitchen counter toward the toaster. I crush it with my middle finger and rinse my hand under the tap. "Are you sure you don't want coffee, Dave?"

"Positive."

"Maybe I'll have some more wine."

After refilling my glass, I set it and the plate of chicken breasts on a tray and flip on the outdoor light.

A pink block wall hides our backyard from the alley and from the backyards of our neighbors: a Vietnamese family who bought just before we did and a 90-year-old widow

<50>

from Missouri who moved in with her husband in 1950, when the development was new. A jade tree hedge grows against the block wall. Dave and I planted a small palm in the middle of the lawn.

I step barefoot along the cold, narrow walk from our kitchen door and stop by our three-legged barbecue grill in moist grass. I dump charcoal into the bowl, squirt on lighter fluid, and toss in a match. A ball of bright orange flame like a small sun lights up the night air. Staring into the flame, I feel hollow inside.

Things aren't always as they appear, I tell myself. The earth appears flat and doesn't feel like it's moving. I try to remember at what age I learned the earth is round and rotating.

We eat in front of *60 Minutes*, and Dave works in his den until bedtime.

In bed, he's tired—not unheard of on a Sunday night. We had sex before we went to Robert's party Friday evening, and again Saturday morning and Saturday night. We kiss, and Dave falls asleep. I fall asleep eventually, an uneasy sleep fret with dreams.

I wake gasping, soaked in sweat. After shoving down my half of the covers, I take deep breaths until my heart stops racing. Tilting my head, I see the red digits glowing *3:07* on the clock radio.

In a slow-motion dream, in a world where air was as dark and sticky as molasses, I was driving head-on at another car with Melinda at the wheel. Sandy was in the front seat, next to Melinda. They were both screaming something at me—a warning—but I couldn't make out what they were saying through our closed car windows.

Dave avoided me at Robert's party, I realize—that's why I didn't have to introduce him to Ian. Ian wants to avoid me as much as he can—that's why he asked for Jack's evening hours. Ian's uncomfortable around me, and not because he's homophobic.

I turn and watch Dave sleeping on his side, facing me. He looks the same as ever, to the naked eye.

<51>

I remember being afraid I'd fly off into space when I first found out the earth was round and spinning at over a thousand miles an hour.

My foot finds Dave's under the covers, my hand touches his. He rouses, lifts his head, and folds a leg over me, stretches an arm across me. His eyes close, his steady breathing resumes.

For the moment, I feel gravity keeping me safe.

<52>

<53>

Adrian Ford

The Airship

conscience hovers over memory's deep
and cold inflowing waves of almost sleep
a gray peripheral
immensity
is all we see
it is so close
in the gondola
no port reveals a human silhouette
and yet
a row of yellow eyes stares at the jet
black water rippling white upon the sand
the little band
that played is gone
the captain at the wheel
invisible
what is it looking for?
footprints leading upward on the sand?
an S.O.S. of driftwood?
our angel, go!
propeller up and back inside the night
our emptiness is better now
and—inside—bright

<54>

Off the Rocks

<55>

Denise Roma

Unus Mundi

My girl rides a bicycle with an alien on the middle bar. She came to the Midwest from England 13 years ago and is still fighting for her green card. Considered an alien but no longer an immigrant.

My girl is, proudly, a 38-year-old teenager, with a faux Mohawk. She is ISOP: In Search of Pussy, with a preference for geek girls because of the innocence—easy to fell saplings with pretty, tender leaves.

My girl is at home on OkCupid tonight looking for someone new. Her personal profile, new as of seven days ago, says she just got out of a relationship in April and is a bad bet to be "your forever girl." The relationship she's talking about has nothing to do with me; she refers here to her 11 years with a Spanish teacher who put her through college so that she could stay in the country. My girl was the teacher's domestic slave in exchange for a liberal arts degree, with no affection or sex in return, the way she tells it.

Her profile says she likes to cook rice and chickpeas and lives in a teeny room, that she is always on a creative spree painting walls and cars and gets the paint all over her cargo shorts. When I was with her, she laced the cargo shorts with a man's leather belt, and I was attracted to both her masculine and feminine qualities: the short, short hair and man's belt, as well as her soft, pale skin and long eyelashes.

My girl is lonely tonight, and it is Saturday.

If I had not loved her so much, we would be reading together on the couch now, her arms around me from behind, a paperback in her hand. She hummed in my ear sometimes, a non-melody that made absolute sense, and I could not have loved her any less.

Unus mundi—Latin for one mind, or one elegant world. We lived in the same elegant world, but my girl was not ready for sustained commitment. My devotion runs hot as

<56>

lava, and she compared that to her own thin rivers, and couldn't keep us afloat. But how I loved to swim in those waters.

We submerged ourselves, entwined underwater, not caring that we weren't breathing air anymore, and then she realized she was in deep. My girl ran back into her shady forest of trees and solitary animals, away from my eyes and skin and arms, and all the possibilities two people create.

Yes, she ran away, she who had once checked for my presence every day. Her calls and e-mails came morning, afternoon, and night. We had set the pattern of her being the boy, pursuing me, and me the girl, receiving her interest.

I hid my own longing behind hers, so that she wouldn't see it and be frightened by my plan of being hers forever. We were joyful together, our hearts glowing in the other's presence, and I couldn't have imagined turning away from that happiness. There was no worry about losing this bright new love, because it was always reaching toward me.

The being away from her now is like the cold bench of a prison, but I have a window to look out of, and the hope of being released. When or where it will come, I don't know, but it was worth it—loving her, the abandonment, the tearing apart, the prison—all worth it.

The first photo my girl sent me was of the top of her head, with her hair carved in the shape of a fish skeleton. I could not see her face. Her arms were extended, and she was dancing. She said to e-mail back if I wanted to see the face that went with the top of her head, and although I was scared by the dead fish, I told her yes. She sent her face in the second photo; it was gentle, with no funny shapes cut into her hair this time. I thought it was a face I could love.

I called the number she provided and was linked to a soft, British voice, someone who had walked around and travelled, like me, and now lived in a college town. We made plans to meet at Starbucks, the way everyone does.

My girl was wearing maroon pants and an okra top for our first meeting, an outfit I would never wear and did not like. She more than made up for the outfit with her soft

<57>

cheek, which I kissed, and snow white skin glowing with her smile, and the way her eyes looked all over my face for me. She was slender and toned from ab crunches, weights, and cardio training, and from loss of appetite after breaking up with her ex. This didn't scare me off. Life had happened to her, the way it had happened to me.

I arrived at my girl's house for our second meeting and found the place populated by the homeowner, a woman who taught kayaking; the timid female law student who rented a room behind a curtain; and the middle-aged man from the second floor who appeared to be ten-years-old. They often ate at a picnic table. The same kind of thrown together family I lived with.

My girl's room was off the kitchen, and contained a cozy bed, computer, desk, and walls adorned with photos of happy times and loved ones. She pulled a helicopter off the top shelf, and we filled it with army men. It had been rescued from the neighborhood trash.

"Do you want to have a fling?" she asked, spinning the propeller.

"I'm not wired for flings," I told her. "I know only how to love another person."

A week and a half later, she e-mailed that she couldn't stop thinking about me, and could try for more than a fling. It was only that she was afraid of the whole "falling in love thing." For me, she would try.

"I could love you," she said the night of the massage, when I saw the fading tattoo of a witch she had gotten as a youth. I don't like witches, I thought. Then I told myself that the tattoo was not an omen, and learned to touch her the way she wanted.

My girl moaned and breathed furiously as I discovered how to give her pleasure.

Her vagina was an alive thing, as all-consuming as a penis, but going inward. I had imagined that a woman would be more subtle, but her sexual longing was just as urgent, like a pulsing heart.

I was amazed by how small her teeth felt when I kissed her. My mind took her in before my body.

<58>

My friend Paul wasn't sure about my girl. He wanted to meet her, and she was well-behaved upon their meeting but did not try to charm him as she did my other friends. She looked past him, pressed her hand against my thigh while he held my other hand and looked worried.

When I spent overnight visits in my girl's room, she let me sleep in the trundle bed that pulled out of hers. She read me bedtime stories about a turtle before turning off the light. We woke up smiling, happy to be together. We made love for hours without looking once at the clock. With the men I had loved, I had enjoyed myself most of the time, but there was the sense of being obligated to fulfill them, and that they were keeping track of the amount of sex we were having. With my girl, I wanted her constantly, the way she wanted me. The tenderness we knew flowed effortlessly between us, like what I had felt with the men, but softer.

We once started out with me seated on a table, my legs wound around her hips, my arms around her neck.

Our kisses ignited something way deep down I had felt only the tip of before, and touched me in every year I had lived.

I sought her as a woman when I kissed her. When I lay my head on her chest, I sought her as a child, and she stroked my hair and understood all of this, and the woman and child integrated as we kissed and touched, and my soul felt like it would burst out of my skin and join with hers.

We moved onto the couch, as I was alone at my writers' studio that day. I climbed on top of her, warmth and passion heightening, and quivered like a startled bird that has just pecked into a new world.

This was the present tense I had sought.

She held me tight wherever we went, and filled me with something I had always ached for: a woman's affection. Even if I lost her, I knew I would remain filled.

What could I give her? I wanted to buy her things: tickets to big shows like *Jersey Boys* that she wouldn't have been able to afford on her artist's pay, dinners out, but she told me that all she wanted was me.

Off the Rocks

<59>

I gave my girl a candle, matches, a coin purse with a pink elephant, and a bar of soap for her birthday. We had been together for one month. It was on this day that she stopped looking me in the eye.

She said she loved me, but that it was a small kind of love; she really had not been ready for any more after all. She just hadn't known it at first.

"We find something beautiful and I want to cherish it, while you want to piss on it," I told her.

My girl was sorry for hurting me, she said, but she couldn't love me in a big way. There was only love, I told her, and it was always big. I stayed at Paul's house and cried for three days, reminding myself of the damn high cost of loving.

My girl was a vampire who sucked my love out of me and then left when she was no longer hungry. She was an angel who gave me everything I had always needed. In the meantime, the sun rises, the sun sets, the way it did in a poem I read as a sophomore.

For the first month or so after parting, I looked for my girl around town, ready to run the moment I found her. She was at a singles event two weeks after our last meeting, and my heart sank to my feet, while she breezed about the room in search of new flesh. She greeted me, but her gentle face was gone.

Not only was I a piece of ass, as my girl assured me via e-mail, but she had so easily moved on, while I had to run from the room once we spotted each other.

I sat down on the sidewalk, letting the tears come. Why did I have to care when she didn't? Of course she hadn't followed me. She was no longer my girl. I was an adolescent compared to her, who had been with many women, had ridden a motorcycle in England, and who would no doubt woo at least someone today with her accent.

But I was lucky that my heart could still fall to my feet over someone, I thought, starting the car. The alternative was meaningless sex, love that burned out and made way for the next partner down the same scorched path.

Off the Rocks

<60>

Unus mundi—one mind, one perfect world together. I cannot smell your skin yet, or see your face, feel your arms gathering me against you, or hear your voice, but you are somewhere, waiting for me, too.

<61>

Anders Krug Waalen

Jason

Your shadow-brushing lashes sweep; your lilting eyes are
laced in mine;
>   *Let me sing thy beast to sleep for fertile fleece of ram
>   divine.*
'Til youth with humor fringed in gray, your hands, in jest
and laughter, steal.
>   *To sail with heroes, monsters slay, though, lover's
>   tragic fate, it seals—*
To fasten fing'rs with such warm ease, from me begs
heartbeats cool, not cold.
>   *Like Hylas lost to Hercules–is to possess... love most
>   bold.*
This flight through thread-thin strait I fail unlike the jokes
of He deemed "straight."
>   *For naiads, God, and princes, sail, but when you
>   leave, just let me hate;*
Perhaps girls giggle not as friends; and men's embraces
simply be;
>   *First mates always fray at ends.... Still–I'll smite thy
>   serpent, set you free,*
Just let me hold your hand in mine. So I can say I had been
thine.

<62>

<63>

Austin Eichelberger

Over Easy

I saw her step into the Pancake House, through the dust-colored glass door and across that faded yellow tile. Her name was Nancy. I had met her years before at a gay club, a few years after my divorce. Now, a little boy toddled along at her side, his hand in hers. She hadn't changed much–same curly brown hair that wouldn't stay back, broad hips and sloping, thin shoulders, little pinched eyes beneath her plucked eyebrows. Not ugly; not beautiful. The boy had big eyes that were a shade of water-blue, almost white around the pupils, and seemed to glow as she walked over and sat him down at the table next to mine. He wore tiny jeans with an elastic waist and a red shirt with a dinosaur on it.

I looked down at my eggs, at the speckled white plate smeared with yolk and ketchup, and for a minute listened to the grinding purr of the open kitchen, the murmurs of the people sitting up at the bar, and some waitress yelling from the back. My grits were halfway gone from the little bowl and the only thing left in my glass of sweet tea was the ice. I figured I was done.

I got up, using my thumb to adjust my sports bra—the one with the seam that bites into my right side—and lit a cigarette slowly. Then I picked up the little blue bill and walked over to Nancy's table.

I don't think she recognized me at first—I've put on some weight and my hair's gone a little grey, plus my skin color is better since I graduated from NA. I got the red keychain and everything. They give you a gold one when you make it a year. It hangs on my keys and I show it to anybody who asks. Nothing to hide.

She looked up at me from the menu; her eyes screwed shut a little bit as the little boy across from her hummed in his highchair and stared at me.

<64>

"It's Nancy, right?" I said as I stuck out my hand. She nodded and shook my hand as her eyes flickered over to the little boy. "I'm Mindy. Remember? From Blaze's? I knew Tommy, that bartender—"

She jumped up then, tossed those almost-too-thick arms around me. I never knew her that well, but I hugged back.

"I didn't even recognize you, it's been forever." She nodded to the little boy, her hand still on my arm. "This here's Tony. Here, you want to sit down?" she asked. She sat back down and smiled up at me.

I slid behind her, pushing the empty chairs at my table in against the plastic tablecloth, and sat on the hard wood of the chair beside her.

Nancy looked over at me. "How are you?"

"I'm doing good, I reckon. Changed a little since my bar days, but I'm good. What've you been up to?"

She looked sideways over at little Tony, still humming away happy as you please and watching me with them blue-white eyes. "Been taking care of this one. He's my niece's son."

"I see." I tapped my cigarette in one of the gold-foil ashtrays they put on each table. I waved smoke away from my face but Nancy didn't seem to mind it. She must be about 40 now—she'd been early thirties when I met her. "I was wondering if he was yours, if you'd found a man or if a man'd found you."

She grinned at me, all teeth and thin lips. "Nope. It sure must have been awhile. You must not remember how I was at the bar."

Truth was, I did. Nancy was one of the girls who would lean too far over the pool table, missing a shot just to stretch out her ass in tight jeans, her mouth small and coy because she knew all the single women like me would stare. The kind of girl who orders drinks for everybody on the tips she got that night. Her hair wasn't as frizzy then, her eyes not as thin and wary.

She looked back over at Tony. He smiled and said, "Momma."

<65>

I puffed on my cigarette and pushed it cherry-first into the little tray. I moved the light metal to the edge of the table with my thumb as a skinny waitress strolled up.

"What do you need to drink?" she asked. "More sweet tea for you, Mindy?"

"Nah." I looked back over at the mess left on my table. "I figure I'm good."

"I'll take a Diet Pepsi and he'll want some apple juice," Nancy told her. The waitress snickered down at Tony, who reached his baby-fat hand out to grab the pen in her short apron. She sidestepped him.

"Be right back with that." The waitress swished away in the green knee-skirt they asked all the girls to wear.

"Did he say Momma?" I asked, thinking of my daughter, her little blond mass of hair and wide, almond-colored eyes. I shifted my cigarettes on the table; the waitress yelped as another waitress spilled Nancy's Diet Pepsi across the kitchen floor.

"Yep. I've had him awhile. He barely remembers his real Momma now—I got him when he was near five months old." She leaned across the table and held the hand he strained out at her, rubbing his sausage fingers with her wide thumb. Her fingers looked soft, like she smoothed them with lotion every night after Tony fell asleep—like she'd been doing that same thing ever since she was a kid.

"What, she didn't pick him up one time?" I plucked another cigarette from the pack and let the box fall back on the table, raising my lighter to my mouth. That first inhale is always the best.

"Nah, I took him from her." Nancy looked at me as she pulled her hand back and I suddenly saw how vivid her hazel eyes were, this shining brown with streaks of leafy green pulling in toward the pupil. They were beautiful.

The waitress set the drinks on the table and lifted her order pad, pen ready. "What would you like?"

Nancy stared down at the menu for a second. "Well, I just want the number six with bacon. And he'll have the kiddie waffles."

The waitress scribbled and nodded, lifted Nancy's menu from the table, and strode back off to the kitchen. Two men

<66>

at the bar looked over at us from under their caps and then went back to pointing at the newspaper spread in front of them. Little Tony curled his hands up and smacked his fists against the table, looking up all surprised-like when they hit.

I leaned in to Nancy. "Do you mean like kidnapping?" I took a long drag from my cigarette and held the smoke in my mouth, letting it creep out slowly.

Nancy laughed, this big, quick guffaw. "Naw, naw. Nothing like that. My niece had this boyfriend—a grown man, I tell you—and he put Tony in the hospital." She cast out her hand for his again. "He was drunk, snatched Tony from the crib one night, and broke both his arms. I couldn't leave family in a place like that, growing up that way." The way she looked over at Tony was tender and shy, like if she looked too hard, the damage the hospital fixed might pop back up again. "He's been my baby ever since I went to that hospital. My niece didn't have a say in the matter, not after I got social services to come see Tony. They handed him straight to me and that was that." Her straw got caught on some bubbles and lifted up, tipping out of the cup toward her. She fixed it between two fingers and sipped, still looking at Tony.

Tony spread his fingers in front of his mouth.

I thought back to when Stacy was a kid, older than Tony, though, when I taught her to rub the cocoa butter on her hands after the bath, slowly in figure eights up her arms and onto her shoulders. Back when I was married, I told myself if I devoted enough time to my husband, I would stop staring at women, would stop watching their move-ments instead of his.

When that didn't work and he caught on, he kicked me out, told the divorce court some bull: that I was cheating, that he was scared for Stacy. When her daddy told me I'd have to leave, I told Stacy to watch the stars for me. "When they twinkle, it means mommy loves you," I'd said. She'd smiled real big and gave me a hug as the crickets made their noise off in the woods.

Then her daddy moved halfway across the country and wouldn't even let me talk to her. He kept the front door

<67>

locked after the first time I came to visit her, would say Stacy was in bed even if I called in the middle of the afternoon. I used to save up my paychecks and drive over there, just watch the lights of the city they lived in from an overlook on the parkway.

Her junior year of high school, she sent me a letter saying she wouldn't send me a school picture because anyone who abandoned her the way I did wasn't worth talking to. She never responded to the letters I sent back; I gave up a few years later, after three or four came back with *No Forwarding Address* stamped in red on the envelopes. She must be out of college by now, on her own; she might even have a kid.

"I'm going to give him a good life, though," Nancy said. "Social services still keeps a quick eye on me. They want to make sure nothing like what happened before happens again." She turned her head back to me, the corduroy over her knee slipping from under the crinkled tablecloth and running into my thigh. My palms were itching like they do when I want to be in the car, driving. "But how are you?" Nancy stared straight at me.

I looked over to the kitchen, at the cook in his backwards grey cap, moping over some omelets behind the grill, at the skinny waitress talking to the two men at the bar and bending to set her elbows on the slick surface. I couldn't tell what they were talking about, but she was laughing and looking into their eyes. "I been good," I said, crushing out my cigarette. "But I have to go, I reckon, got to meet somebody uptown for a minute." I stood, even though I didn't have anybody to see. "It was nice to catch up. I hope Tony isn't too much for you. They can be."

She smiled again. "Yep, but it's worth it. They're worth it."

"Yeah," I said. I squeezed between the chairs again, my cigarettes and crumpled bill in one hand, and shook her hand from the end of the table. "I'll see you."

Her mouth moved like she wanted to say something, like she had a question, but it went still as I turned for the cash register. As the waitress rang me up, I pulled singles out of my thin wallet and handed them over when she stuck her

<68>

hand out. Then I turned and walked in shaky steps to the dingy glass door and the burning sunlight outside.

<69>

Tyler Gillespie

Granville

The corner store on Granville and Winthrop is
the cheapest place I've found to buy cigarettes in Chicago.
$7.56 a pack for Marlboro Lights–
two dollars more than in Florida–
but $1.50 less than on Clark Street or in downtown.

When I moved to Chicago
I promised myself that I'd quit
smoking,
but instead
I've found the cheapest cigarettes.

The corner store is close to the
Gerber/Hart Library
(the neighborhood LGBT library that I heard has plans to
move to Clark Street)
and the Granville Anvil
(the seedy gay bar where people go for quick sex and cheap
drinks).
These two places are neighborhood hangouts.

The corner store only lets you pay in cash–
unless you make a $10 purchase,
which is equivalent to two packs of cigarettes–
around $15 at this point.

When I moved to Chicago
I promised myself I'd quit smoking,
but I always buy two packs of cigarettes
when I don't have any cash on me.

<70>

<71>

B.M. Spaethe

You're So Skin Tight

-after the Scissor Sisters

The evening passes through the three of us,
Justin lifts his chin to O smoke from his mouth
& Jacob says, *Let's go to 501*, where we slip

in wearing t-shirts & tight, tight jeans, the place bearing
rainbow flags like the last. I hold my
bowler hat against my head, protecting it from fans

blowing near large men in tight, leather shorts,
chains strapped crossways over their chests.
They must have missed the small mounds protruding

beneath my shirt. I'm standing in the back when a man
asks, *Are you okay?* as if to say, *You know this
is a place for men, right?* as if to say, *You aren't*

looking in the dark pool room under televisions
stuck in the corner: blinking one naked man
after another over the wet look of black paint on the walls,

& wobbly tables against them under mirrors,
where I tuck the genitals that don't hang below
my belt back between my legs & let my bare chest

sweat through a black mesh shirt, pull the leotard
wedge from my ass while leaning over a table, & smear
dark lipstick down my face. Justin takes my

hat from my head, putting it on his head, & Jacob slides
my glasses up the bridge of his nose, both
sipping on their hot pink cocktail straws, posing

<72>

with cigarettes for blurred photos, my neon green
straw, bit between my teeth, all of us blurring into one
waving caterpillar dressed as if macramé and paper maché

one of us sitting in the corner, glaring down into a phone,
one of us leaning back on the pool table, heels up,
one of us coming out of the dark bathroom where the glory
holes are winked through.

<73>

Barry Frauman

San Francisco

Open sky, city of rangy vistas
built mostly close to ground:
Golden Gate Bridge of harp-strung reach,
its twin majestically spanning the bay
near long, broad piers of Fisherman's Wharf
which see the water at different slants
amid its shops and seafood dining.
South of the Wharf, a spacious park
rises hilly toward this town
of sidewalk steps for headier climbs.

The Castro, hub of alternative sex,
boutiques and bars and cinema:
Classics of the silver screen
regale us with Bette Davis, James Dean,
Cary Grant, Hollywood's golden age.

The Gay Pride Parade, vast march up Market Street
into the Castro:
Gaudily made-up drag queens bask
in cascading wigs and super-long eyelashes;
leather-leg jock straps sport bare asses;
Dykes on Bikes alone equal
total paraders anywhere else.

Neighboring residential hills
tout Painted Ladies,
three-story houses done outside
in brilliant purples, yellows, greens.

Cable cars clang up and down
the highest peaks of town.
Dizzying zigzag Lombard Street:
Not knowing its infamous repute,

<74>

my aunt drove us quick down its numerous curves,
half a rollercoaster delight.

Steep Columbus Avenue,
Corso Cristoforo Colombo,
Restaurant Row of Italian touch,
old-country cooks and waiters,
hailing distance from Chinatown
where streets are Asian analog.

The War Memorial Opera House,
Beaux-Arts structure of medium scale,
a troupe in splendid performances
of musical drama masterworks,
traditional and avant garde as well.

The city itself is middle size;
bigness and quality do not always....

<75>

O.C. Devanney

Personal and Political

This is a memoir of lesbian life in Boston in the mid '80s. This excerpt focuses on the fall of 1987, the time of the Second National March on Washington for Lesbian and Gay Rights.

On Saturday, October 10, we traveled down to D.C. I felt nervous about meeting Ginny, who would be driving. I hoped she'd be cute. She wasn't, though she might have been cute if she hadn't weighed over 250 pounds. Although it was six in the morning when Ginny picked me up, she seemed friendly and good-humored. She smiled at me from behind her round, wire-rimmed glasses and said in her Southern accent, "We have to go get my honey Catherine now. I sure hope she got some sleep. She's been studying a lot. She's a medical student."

"A medical student?"

"Yup. Would you like a donut hole or a coffee?" Ginny popped a jelly donut hole, then a chocolate one into her mouth, and brandished a Dunkin' Donuts bag.

"No thanks to the donuts. But I'd love a coffee." I reached into the back and extracted a cup from a four-pack on the floor. *Damn!* I thought to myself as I sucked on my hot, creamy coffee. *How did this woman score a med student and I can't get a date to save my life?* This Catherine must be ugly and old. Probably really huge. I knew I was being lookist, ageist, and sizeist, but it was too early in the morning to scold myself into better thoughts.

"Could you run up and ring the doorbell and let Catherine know we're here?" asked Ginny as we pulled up. I jogged to the white-painted wooden door, which opened just as I was about to rap on it, revealing an attractive woman in her early thirties. She had short blond hair and slightly goofy glasses, but she was presentable. At this

<76>

point in my two-year marathon of celibacy, I'd have gone on a date with her happily. Like a shot.

Catherine was carrying a couple of big science text-books. Before getting into the backseat, she leaned into the open passenger side car door and she and Ginny kissed in a chaste sort of way.

"Hi, honey!"

"Hi, sweetheart! How are you?"

"Want me to get in back?" I asked.

"No, don't worry," said Catherine. "You stay in front with Ginny. I have to study, anyway."

We drove to the Fenway Neighborhood to pick up the third and fourth passengers. "We're getting my ex Jo and her sister Teresa now," explained Ginny. Again, I anticipated a couple of lumpy, middle-aged women in over-tight chinos and pilled sweaters. Ginny pulled up outside an old red brick building and honked.

After a moment, a thin girl who looked like a handsome, scruffy adolescent boy emerged from a basement apart-ment. She was smoking a Marlboro and wore a faded denim jacket. Her short hair was pale reddish-gold and her black Converse sneakers were splashed with paint, as were the thin knuckles protruding from her thready denim cuffs. I got out of the car, staring at her fine features, her clear, freckled skin, and her dark eyebrows and lashes. Catherine had been perfectly adequate, but Jo was more than adequate. She was hot. I looked at Ginny out of the corner of my eye, wondering. The whole thing seemed inexplicable.

"Honey..." whined Catherine from the backseat.

"No smoking in the car, Jo! Where's Teresa?"

"Teresa's getting a ride with another friend." Jo's voice was low and attractive. She dropped her cigarette and stamped on it, and just as I was beginning to feel disapproving, she kicked the butt tidily down a storm drain. Then she got into the car and fell asleep.

It was eight hours to Washington, but the time passed fairly quickly, even though Ginny pulled into highway rest stops to eat every two and a half hours. The highway down was lined almost exclusively with Roy Rogers, a fast food burger place I had read of once in a novel, but never seen before. The food was quite disgusting, but Ginny bought sturdy hot beef sandwiches, fries, and giant cups of Coke and consumed them deftly, one hand on the wheel. Between meals, she broke into friendly chatter, and told me Jo was an artist. Every now and then I swung around to glance at Jo and ask her questions, but the angle was hard on my neck, so I couldn't make eye contact as much as I wanted to.

"I'd love to see some of your work," I said.

"Sure. Anytime."

"Are you an art student?"

"Not anymore. I was at Pratt in New York, but I dropped out. I work at a restaurant on Newbury Street called Rudi's. The owner's this temperamental French woman, Sabine."

"How's Sabine treating you these days, Jo?" asked Catherine.

"Okay. But she just fired one of the *sous*-chefs. You know, she's usually nice to me. She likes me because I was born in France. Plus, she likes flirting with me, even though she's straight."

"Really? Do you speak French?" I asked.

"I did when I was little, but we only stayed in Paris until I was four. My parents are English."

When we got to D.C., Ginny dropped me on a street corner and I took the Washington Metro out to the suburbs, where I was staying for the night. I was amazed at the Metro's cleanliness and wide concrete spaces. I decided the T was cozier, more genuine, built on a human scale, like the wandering streets of Boston. Standing on the grey cement Metro platform, I surreptitiously ate one of Ginny's donut holes. The Transit Authority had posted signs forbidding food, and I took them seriously. I reflected as I chewed that D.C. was the belly of the bureaucratic American beast. I felt a sudden affection for Boston, where I could drink early morning coffee on the Red Line as I sped to my menial job. Nobody cared. In Boston, I could probably order a pizza delivery to Park Street T Station, and feed my crumbs to the little grey mice that ran along the rails. Massachusetts was and always would be the Cradle of Liberty.

Journal Entry: Saturday, October 10

I'm staying the night with my Wesleyan friend Ruth at her brother Michael's place. He and his dumpy wife—who is very intelligent and speaks about five languages, including Russian—share a Bethesda ranch house with another couple. All four of them work for the same agency in Washington. They bought the house together and eat dinner together most nights; it's like a conservative geek commune. Michael went to MIT. During dinner I asked Michael which agency they worked for. I got this long, convoluted answer which didn't tell me anything at all. Thinking of Philip Agee, I laughed and said, "What, you guys don't all work for The Company or anything, do you?" Long, awkward silence.

Journal Entry: Sunday, October 11

The march today was, for me, a typical crazy-making crowd scene. Just now, I have half an hour before meeting Ginny and the others for my ride back to Boston. I am taking the time to sit under a tree on The Mall and transcribe a little sanity. I am so insecure. I have no skin at all, and this makes me terribly unhappy.

Ruth and I walked with the Wesleyan contingent, and as usual I felt shy and out of place. It's only been 16 months since I graduated. Not much has changed. I saw Rachel Venning. My heart hammered the moment I caught sight of her schoolboy profile. When I think of how I feel about Rachel, how I felt about Liz at work and about my old Women's Studies professor—when I think of how I feel about all of these women, who in truth are strangers but who matter so much, I want to die from desire and frustration.

<79>

Women ignore me, but men don't leave me alone, and I hate it. Maybe I should chop off all my long hair, but I love my hair. Rather than enjoying life, I am clambering through a hellish wreckage of bones and desiccated thorns. It is as though there's an oasis somewhere (or is it a mere mirage?) but I cannot touch it.

After 16 months, Rachel still dries my mouth and speeds my pulse as though I had just seen lightning strike the ground in front of me. She makes my hands shake and turns my self-consciousness up full volume. I feel as though my desire is visible, as though the irrational force of my feelings shines out of me like an aura. All I need to do is see her profile and I feel as though I've taken five hits of nitrous. Rachel doesn't even see me. She gazes over my head.

I have a good distraction, though, because during the ride down here I developed a crush on one of my fellow passengers, Jo. She is a painter, and lives in a basement apartment on Hemenway in the Fens. She shares it with rats and her 1270 Club bartender/bouncer sister, Teresa. I saw Teresa and Jo briefly at the march today. Teresa is about six feet tall and strongly built with a platinum-blond flat top. She's very pretty, but she looks like she could kick your ass. She dresses all in black, from her Doc Marten boots to her turtleneck sweater, and wears heavy black eye make-up. Jo's so different from Teresa. Jo's small and thin with sandy hair, freckles, and dark eyelashes. She's both cool and nerdy.

Two days after the March on Washington, I asked Jo out. I went to Newbury Street, and walked into Rudi's, where she worked. Rudi's was bright, Parisian, and trendy with shining black-and-white tile floors. Delicious salads, cakes, and baked savories filled the spotless stainless steel cases. Jo was standing behind the counter in a white men's undershirt and white apron. I felt half excited and half repelled by the slight gold shimmer on her upper lip. She wore a chain and labrys around her neck. I was afraid I

<80>

would not be able to open my mouth and speak; my heart
hammered and the blood flooded my face. Jo looked
relaxed and pleased to see me. She said she'd be glad to go
to the movies with me and scribbled her phone number on
a Rudi's bag. Having risked so much by asking her out, I
felt like a peeled shrimp, all exposed and ready to curl up.

Journal Entry: Thursday, October 15

I want a lover so badly. I want, once again, to taste
another's breath, to slide my hands over another's bones.
But that seems so insurmountably difficult. I want magic,
but the hope of magic leads to overwhelming feelings and,
ergo, fear. Fear gets in my way. Sex is no use without
magic. If there is no magic, there's nothing. But if there is
the hope of a good sexual spell, I can hardly speak to the
other.

An aside: since I've been sleeping on a bare box spring for
over a year, I find my new futon shockingly comfortable. I
can hardly get up in the morning. I feel as though I'm
sleeping surrounded by warmth and feathers, like an egg in
a down-lined nest. Maybe Jo will sleep there with me. I
suppose I'm not sorry to feel as I do about her. Even if my
desire leads to rejection and humiliation, it's been worth it.
I feel intensely alive.

Tuesday, October 20

   Back in the real world, the stock market has crashed
worse than Black Thursday of '29. Good. Maybe something
will finally happen. Like the end of the world economy as
we know it? I doubt it, though. The big boys seem to have
everything under control. As usual.
   Exactly two weeks after the March on Washington, Jo
and I went out. I waited for her outside the Kenmore
Square T Station. Teresa and her clandestine girlfriend
dropped Jo off in a large, silver-blue Chevrolet sedan with
CT plates. It was strange to see Teresa leaning out the
parental sedan window with her flat top and her attitude.

<81>

Jo and I went for coffee before the movie. We sat in an old Jewish-style deli, drank coffee out of thick white china cups, and listened to the mini jukebox. I could hardly focus on what she was saying—I was too keyed up.

As we sat opposite each other in the dark wood of the booth, I noticed Jo's thin hands. Her skin was pale pink and translucent, and her hair a fine reddish-gold, but her lashes and eyebrows were dark. I could not meet her gaze for long—she was too beautiful—but I noticed that her eyes were curiously colored: the right one was three quarters green and one quarter amber.

We paid and left, and I locked my bicycle to a road sign. During our walk to the Nickelodeon Cinema, I felt horribly self-conscious. When we settled in the tipped red velvet seats of the theater, I was hyper-aware of how we were positioned, of her forearm and shoulder next to mine. Then I got lost in the film.

Journal Entry: Monday, October 26

I saw a film, *I've Heard the Mermaids Singing*, with Jo. I think that's a line from T.S. Eliot. As I watched, I nearly wept. That must sound trite, but I found the film so evocative. It was about a woman who falls in love with another woman. The protagonist was ordinary, and rather awkward, but she was heroic and beautiful as well. She was transfigured by her love and her art. I thought the film was about the mundaneness and pettiness of life, and the unattainable purity of... something—the something varies depending on who you are. The heroine was a photographer, a brilliant photographer, but she lacked money or connections, and she worked as a secretary in a gallery. She had to make her art on the weekends and after work, like Jo and me. Her photographs were the most beautiful art in the film, and yet they were not acknowledged or appreciated, so the film was about unfairness, nepotism, and "artistic success." As I watched the film, I sighed from an excess of feeling, and from lust for Jo.

<82>

After the film, we walked to the 1270 Club on Boston Road where Teresa (or Tee, as Jo calls her) bartends and bounces. I'm not sure how well we connect, Teresa and me. She strikes me as an intellectually uncomplicated party girl, though she said something sophisticated-sounding about the great cinematography in *I've Heard the Mermaids Singing*. What is cinematography exactly? Filming technique? For me, film is all about plot, character, and dialog. Teresa is being nice to me, but is she nice really? Is there any depth beyond the tough glamour and flash of Tee?

At the 1270, Tee gave us beer on discount, and I didn't know whether I should tip. She bent her head to kiss me on greeting, and I didn't know which cheek to turn, so I did a sort of chicken-headed incomplete shuffle. Felt like a complete idiot, especially in the face of Tee's barroom cool. Then Jo and I went downstairs and talked for three hours. The 12 is dark, gloomy, and modern with hard-edged black fittings and thumping house music, but it all faded away as we sat on the industrial iron stairs and talked. I didn't even miss dancing, and I love to dance. Jo doesn't dance. Ever.

We left and she walked to Mass Ave with me. I kissed her goodbye on the cheek. Her face felt smooth and cold. She said, "Give me a call," and I said I would. My only dilemma is what to invite her to do. I wonder how she feels about me. She didn't make any kind of physical pass. I think that's going to be my job.

A total aside: I went to a used clothing store today. I was drawn, as always, to the black cashmere fur-collared coats, the narrow-waisted black dresses, and the patterned stockings. Do I have femme tendencies? I couldn't wear those clothes really, not with my life, but they are so beautiful. I don't look good in men's clothes; I'm too curvy. I sure can wear women's clothes, though, especially women's clothes from the thirties and forties.

<83>

I worked as a florist at Bread and Circus, and the Monday after the movie, I considered buying Jo a gardenia bush from my department. The leaves of the plant were dark and polished; the creamy whorls of flower gave off an odor that was nearly too sweet. I inhaled the white flowers and felt high. The sensation matched the lightheadedness I felt when I saw Jo. I considered that it was the perfect present, everything I wanted to do with her, every sweetness incarnate in a plant. But $25 was one eighth of my paycheck.

That night, my friend Ruth and I went to the 1270, half looking for Jo. We felt very crunchy granola on the basement dance floor, the lone hippy chicks in a crowd of gay and lesbian monochrome fashionistas. We each drank a couple of beers, then tried to imitate the other dancers by rocking really close, knees between knees, to the thumping four-four rhythm of house. We didn't see Jo, but her sister Teresa was working as a bouncer.

Tee was standing on the metal stairs, scanning the room. With her height and her position, she stood out above the crowd like a queen. She was dressed all in black as usual, and had cut her hair again. The sides were shaved down to dark fuzz, but the longer hair at the crown remained platinum blond. I had never seen a two-tone flat top before. As Tee lounged on her feet, all coolness and bravado, I realized she turned me on a little with her mild dominatrix energy, scary and sexy at the same time. She radiated so much attitude that when she deigned to acknowledge Ruth and me, we felt humble and grateful. "Teresa," said Ruth, "is club royalty."

Journal Entry: Sunday, November 1

Alice Pomeroy from Wesleyan stayed for a few days, but now she's gone. She's headed for Denver for a Social Work internship. She brought her new girlfriend, who is over 40 and fresh out of a 20-year het marriage. Alice remains her sturdy, golden-brown lioness self, and I love her.

<84>

Saturday the three of us went out to a Halloween event at the Somerville Theatre. Wall to wall jubilant lesbians. Not a man in the house. We listened to Mary Daly, Sonia Johnson, Alix Dobkin, and this incredible duo, Casselberry-DuPreé. I'm going to buy their album. They brought the house down, two dreadlocked women, one tall and golden, one small and nearly black, both dressed in African-print clothes. Casselberry-DuPreé invoked the orisha, the Yoruba deities, at the beginning of their concert and then closed with a sealing invocation. The female spiritual energy in that room, between Halloween and Casselberry-DuPreé—I thought the theatre was going to levitate! My favorite song was called "Did Jesus Have a Baby Sister?"

Ruth and Charley Foulks and I met for coffee afterwards, and Ruth told us about her date with Kirin, an older woman she met at the AIDS quilt after the March on Washington. Kirin's a biker, with short blond hair, glasses, and a leather jacket. She doesn't appeal to me at all, but I'm not Ruth. I guess the AIDS quilt was quite the pickup scene. Apparently Barb Martineau from Wesleyan met some woman there and the connection was so hot they went and got a room. Over the cookies and coffee, Charlie kept going on and on about how tacky Barb was, picking somebody up at the AIDS quilt. Sour grapes! Sex and death. They kind of go together, don't they? Amidst Death we are in Life and all that. Like the Irish wake. You need to prove you're alive after someone dies, and what better way than drinking uproariously and/or fucking?

Jo and I got together a week later. She was my first female lover and she was everything I had imagined.

I let her down in the end, because I was hungry for experience and tempted by other women.
Although I lived the lesbian life for another decade, I never met anybody like Jo.
Of them all, I loved her best.

<85>

Sarah Fonseca

On Dating a Jewish Girl

I could never pinch
her cheeks
It reminded me
Of winter's cruel cold
Of searchlights,
Of barking dogs and
SS officers
Of her ancestors standing
in line for sorting
At Auschwitz,
Clutching luggage and
Loved ones
Grabbing the turgid skin
Of their faces,
Twisting hard,
trying their best
to look alive
while feeling
while smelling
death

I did not pinch but
I tickled, evoking
Not pain
But laughter
Not *Sophie's Choice*
But *Pee-wee's Playhouse*

<86>

Off the Rocks

<87>

Vince Sgambati

Forgiveness

From the mirror over a dresser, a stranger peers at Lena through milky slits, and her scant black hair, gray at the roots, and withered, mottled flesh, conjure up memories of ancient Italian donnas pawing vegetables and fruit or sniffing fish from pushcarts along Second Avenue, and—more vividly—memories of the crone in South Beach who years ago yelled at Lena and her sister and cousins because the children danced outside of her bungalow singing, "When your hair has turned to silver..." She called them dirty little wops, and the very young Lena shouted back: "You have a face like a fried egg!"

Lena lifts a photograph from the dresser: a faint pyramid of family with her grandmother at the crown, embraced by daughters, daughters-in-law, and grand-children in front of the rambling summerhouse with the wide, screened-in porch and cascading hydrangeas. Her generous father rented this house in South Beach, Staten Island, so that the family's women and children could escape the hot flats in Harlem; husbands and fathers joined them via railroad and Staten Island Ferry on week-ends or on Sunday afternoons and evenings after they closed their shops. She spots herself in the photograph and is hard-pressed to reconcile the young girl with big eyes and thick black curls resting her head on her grand-mother's aproned knee with the old timer staring back at her from the mirror. "Can't be," Lena whispers.

Rosaries, prayer cards, a jewelry box, hairbrush, and toilet articles clutter the dresser. Her things, but why are they here and why are they dusted with bath powder? Why are her family photographs displayed, and why is she wearing a nightgown, and why is the stranger in the mirror wearing the identical nightgown? And who is this ancient stranger that glares at her so critically?

<88>

Lena's son will know. He's upstairs. She's not sure why he's upstairs, but she knows he is, unless he's already gone home... but he wouldn't do that... he wouldn't leave her. That she's sure of. She lifts a robe from the unmade bed and leaves the room that's not her bedroom, though it contains so many of her things.

"Charlie... Charlie..." He wakes slowly to his mother's plea, distant and frail. Not the emphatic tone of the mother who once summoned him home—from up the block or across the street—for dinner or to finish his homework or, on sticky summer nights when teenagers ruled stoops and negotiated pecking orders until all hours, she, like so many mothers—tired of crossword puzzles or television or magazines or novenas—called out to her teenager through an open window onto a city street because she couldn't sleep until he was home.

"I'm coming, Ma," he hears himself reply, but in his half-awake state he's unsure if he answers the mother in the downstairs dining room turned bedroom or the mother calling her son home long ago.

In the dim light and from his vantage at the top of the stairs looking down on her, she appears elfin, like a child with progeria.

"Charlie, what are we doing here? Let's go home. We don't belong here."

Finger to his lips. "Shh... you'll wake Rochelle." He rushes down the stairs and ushers Lena back into her bedroom, which is directly below Rochelle's, then pulls the French doors closed behind them. Lena's wearing her hearing aids, so Charlie speaks softly, but mouths his words like a silent movie actor. "You are home."

"This isn't a house; it's a shop, like Daddy's grocery or Grandpa's butcher," Lena insists.

Not again, Charlie worries. His parents moved up from Queens ten years ago after his father's dementia had become too advanced for his mother to care for him alone. Charlie's partner agreed to have them move in, and for the next year, until a major stroke ended Frank's life, Charlie and Michael spent many nights deterring Frank from unlocking doors or climbing out windows, or lifting him

Off the Rocks

<89>

after falls and quieting his nightly rants and cleaning up piss and shit. They also had the second-floor hardwoods carpeted to muffle sound so that at least three-year-old Rochelle's sleep wasn't disrupted and she wasn't frightened. After Frank passed, they turned the dining room into a bedroom—Lena had difficulty climbing stairs—and renovated the first floor half-bathroom into a full bathroom with laundry facilities, and Lena has lived with them ever since.

"Ma, this is our house and these are your things." Charlie's hand sweeps the room. Lena stands frozen like the cat Charlie once saved from being crushed on a highway. Not much traffic, so he pulled over, waved cars away, and whisked the catatonic animal to the side of the road. Moments passed before the cat shook off its stupor and disappeared into the weeds.

And moments pass before Lena nods and responds: "But I don't understand... You won't leave me... will you, Charlie?"

"Of course I won't leave you, Ma, but please get back in bed. You don't want to wake Rochelle, do you? She's sleeping. It's very late. I promise that I won't leave you."

Charlie pulls the bedcovers up around his mother's shoulders. If only he could wipe the foreshadowing of dementia from her eyes. He recalls his father crumbling in a recliner with an afghan tucked around him, even though it was August. Frank wore his vacant expression that morphed into confusion then back again, like a hologram of mental decline. Rochelle, barely three, played patty cake with her grandfather's trembling hand as if her grandfather deserved her affection, but who's to judge what someone else deserves?

"Promise me, Charlie, you won't leave without me," Lena pleads.

"I promise you, Mom. I'll still be here in the morning and we'll talk like always," Charlie answers. As he opens the French doors, he thinks to sit awhile in the living room, outside his mother's bedroom, but then sees Rochelle at the top of the stairs, her knees tucked up under her chin and her piano fingers clasped in front of her shins. A few

<90>

steps up and he smiles and strokes her cheek. "Hey, baby...
you okay?"

"I guess so. Grandma?"

"Probably had a bad dream, but she's okay now."

"Is Daddy home yet?"

"No, he's working a double shift. He'll be home in the
morning."

Charlie follows Rochelle into her room. She climbs into
bed and he helps pull up her bedcovers. "Poppy, could you
stay with me for a little while?"

"Sure, baby." He lies down next to her and with his three
middle fingertips traces figure eights on Rochelle's arm,
but he feels guilty about leaving his mother alone.

Two weeks ago, while Lena stood at the kitchen counter
eating cereal, milk dribbled from the corner of her mouth
down her chin. Charlie asked her if she felt all right and she
nodded, but after finishing her breakfast, Lena complained
that she felt lightheaded and wanted to go sit in her room.
Even though Charlie suspected that Lena was suffering a
slight stroke or something worse, he dismissed thoughts of
calling an ambulance. She had long been fearful of doctors
and hospitals, not to mention nursing homes.

In recent years her fears worsened—just the mention of a
doctor's appointment brought on sleepless nights with
bouts of diarrhea. "I'm almost a hundred. Leave me alone,"
she argued. Better she should pass sitting in her room,
watching a favorite movie with her son nearby, rather than,
as Lena often sputtered, "in one of those places with
strangers." He grew up hearing her preach: "One mother
can care for five children, but five children can't care for
one mother." No siblings to call, but he had Michael and
Rochelle and lots of DVDs. Thank God for Julia Roberts
and Sandra Bullock.

Once in her room, Charlie helped his mother sit and
asked if she felt better. She smiled and nodded. For the
next few days, Lena slurred her words and complained that
she had trouble walking. By day five, she was back to
herself as if nothing had happened. Tonight, with
Rochelle's head against his chest, he worries that Lena's
confusion might be from another little stroke and that

<91>

Lena will ultimately experience firsthand what his father had gone through. TMIs are what the doctor called them, and while tracing figure eights on his daughter's arm, Charlie hopes that his mother is asleep, not struggling to make sense of her strange bedroom or fearing that her son will leave without her.

Unlike the South Beach crone with the fried egg face, Lena enjoys young people. On weekday mornings, while the teenagers wait outside for the school bus, Lena watches Rochelle through her bedroom window, but she's careful not to rustle the drapes for fear that she might embarrass her granddaughter—too late to be the grandmother she had hoped to be, lively and indispensable like her grandmother and mother had been.

Slow-moving and precarious, Lena mostly stays out of the way, especially on school mornings when Rochelle storms through the kitchen, grabbing breakfast, her schoolbooks, and her coat. Once Rochelle is outside with her friends, Lena admires her through lace drapes. Rochelle is tall and slender with almond-shaped eyes and a pecan complexion. "You resemble that singer. You know who I mean. Whitney something," Lena repeats at least once a week, and Rochelle responds with a smile that Lena reads as tolerance. Not that she faults her granddaughter; after all, Lena knows that she repeats herself and her hearing is poor and she probably misspeaks more often than she realizes.

Like once at the dinner table when Charlie and Michael and Rochelle debated politics and Lena mused aloud, "I wonder if I'll live to see a woman president." If only she had stopped there, but then she shrugged her shoulders and said, "Who knows? After all, now we have a colored president." Conversation ceased, and she knew she said something wrong but could barely remember what it was she had said. Later, Charlie berated her for her choice of words. Even though she was taken aback by Charlie's reaction—after all, hadn't she heard Charlie's friends say "people of color"?—she apologized to Rochelle and as always, Rochelle smiled, even gave her a hug, but Lena

<92>

wasn't convinced. "I think Rochelle might be a little resentful of the attention you give me," Lena often confided in Charlie, but Charlie dismissed her concern with: "You know how kids are."

So Lena stands near the windows in her bedroom and imagines her granddaughter talking to her the way she goes on and on with her friends, the way Lena once went on and on with her sister and cousins. Then the teenagers disappear into a yellow school bus and Lena waves good-bye behind the lace drapes. Her doors open into the kitchen and Charlie sits on a stool at the counter, sipping coffee and reading the morning paper.

"Good morning. How are you feeling?" he asks.

There's the familiar whistle, like a train entering a tunnel, as Lena presses her red fingernail against her hearing aid and adjusts the volume.

"I said how are you feeling?" Charlie raises his voice.

"Good," Lena answers then hobbles to the pantry.

"What was that all about last night?"

"I don't know. I was a little confused, but I'm fine now. Sometimes I'm more in the next world than this one." With one hand, she carries a box of cereal, and her other hand presses against the top of the kitchen counter. Charlie brings her a bowl, and she rests the box on the counter and grabs two handfuls of cereal, dropping some in the bowl and some on the floor, where the Schnoodle in waiting is rewarded. Next, Lena soaks her cereal with half and half.

Charlie chuckles. "Lena's diet for a long life: half and half and chocolate."

"That reminds me." She brings a shaky spoon to her mouth. "I'm all out of chocolate."

"Didn't Michael just buy some when he went shopping?"

"All gone." Lena smiles sheepishly.

Charlie shakes his head. "Then you start crying and want to know why you have such bad diarrhea. Your big C is chocolate, not cancer."

She nods. Sounds of Lena's spoon tapping the bowl, until she scoops up the last of the cereal then carries the bowl to the sink. She opens the dishwasher and slowly removes the clean dishes one at a time, laboriously drying

<93>

some with a paper towel then stacking them on the counter below the cupboards.

After the clean dishes are put away and the dirty ones are loaded into the dishwasher, she'll shower and get dressed, followed by rosaries, a DVD or two–that she'll mostly sleep through–and reading and crossword puzzles, though over the past year or two, Lena spends much less time doing crossword puzzles and for the most part rereads the same three or four books and watches the same movies over and over: *Moonstruck, Princess Diaries, Guys and Dolls*, and anything with Julia Roberts or Sandra Bullock. Language from some of these movies, especially considering Lena's television volume, has caused embarrassing questions, like the time five-year-old Rochelle asked Lena what a blowjob is. Several of Julia Roberts's movies took a brief hiatus until Rochelle got older.

"Here, Ma, take your medicine." Lena's startled by Charlie's voice. He hands her three pills, one at a time, and she alternates the pills with sips of water. After the dog had suffered a seizure and Charlie discovered a pill on Lena's bedroom carpet, he showed her the incriminating evidence and took charge of dispensing medicine.

The dog barks, followed by Michael's voice. Lena adjusts the train whistle in her hearing aid and Michael joins them in the kitchen.

"Good morning."

Lena looks up from the opened drawer of silverware to Michael's smile. She likes Michael. "Like a second son," she says. His cheery manner, a quality that Lena suspects makes him a good nurse, put her at ease the first time she met him almost 25 years ago. Frank also liked him and they were always hospitable when Charlie brought Michael to their house, even after years passed and Frank began whispering to Lena: "I think they're boyfriends," and Lena told Frank to get his mind out of the gutter.

"Good morning," Lena answers. She can't help but notice that her son remains silent and busies himself pouring another cup of coffee, even though he never drinks more than one cup at breakfast, but it's none of her business.

<94>

"Gonna grab a shower. Got a minute, Charlie?"

Charlie's eyes remain glued to his cup of coffee. "I'll be up."

Lena glances at her son. She hadn't noticed or she'd forgotten how much gray had replaced the black in his hair. She continues to dry the perfectly dry silverware.

His back against a mountain of pillows, Charlie's sitting up in bed reading when Michael enters the room dripping wet, a towel wrapped around his waist. No need for Charlie to look up. In his mind's eye, he can see—not the young body he explored 25 years ago, but Michael stays in fairly good shape and there's something to be said for maturity.

"I told Rochelle you worked a double shift last night," Charlie says, rereading the same page.

Michael searches the underwear drawer, his towel drops, and Charlie's eyes respond, looking over his reading glasses and following Michael's damp back down to the swell of his buttocks. They haven't been together in weeks, for them a long time. *Where the fuck were you last night?* Charlie thinks. *Double shift, my ass.* He finds Michael's silence unsettling. "My mom woke us last night. I think it scared Rochelle."

"Is she okay?" Michael slips on a pair of jeans, but leaves them unzipped.

"I think Rochelle is okay, but something is going on with my mom. She's getting worse, you know."

Charlie closes his book and Michael sits at the foot of the bed and rests his hand on Charlie's leg. Sunlight catches the dew on Michael's beard and chest and arms. He leans forward, his hand moving up Charlie's leg and his lips so close that Charlie feels Michael's breath against his face.

"I'm sorry," Michael whispers.

"For what?"

"For everything," Michael answers, and he presses his full body against Charlie's and Charlie doesn't resist.

After Charlie follows Michael upstairs, Lena lifts Charlie's empty coffee mug from the counter and turns it upside down in the dishwasher. She worries that there's a

<95>

problem between the boys. The house is filled with photographs of Charlie and Michael's life together, anniversaries are celebrated, Christmas and birthday gifts are exchanged with a kiss, Rochelle calls the men Poppy & Daddy–there are countless examples that point to the fact that Charlie and Michael are a couple, but Charlie has never actually discussed this with Lena–at least not in so many words.

After several years of Charlie bringing Michael down to the house in Queens for visits, including occasional holidays, Lena and Frank stopped asking Charlie if he had a girlfriend or if he hoped to ever marry, and when Rochelle came along they assumed that just Charlie had adopted her. They didn't know that two men could adopt together. Frank would make comments to Lena–sometimes concerned, sometimes cruel–about the boys, but Lena was a pro at ignoring what she didn't want to hear or see. Twenty years ago she would have loved for Charlie and Michael to go their separate ways, but now the prospect saddens her. And her sadness lingers while she showers and dresses and she becomes weepy as she says her morning prayers. *Moonstruck* is a great antidote for sadness, but Lena soon falls asleep to Cher telling Danny Aiello that he must propose to her on his knees if he expects them to marry.

She wakes to a blank TV screen and the sound of her granddaughter's voice. No way that Lena's going to make it to the bathroom in time, so she opens the bottom drawer of her dresser and removes a pair of disposable adult underpants–utilitarian, bulky, and distasteful to a woman who once sewed lace on her already fancy undergarments. Usually careful to wrap the used, damp, sometimes soiled underpants in a small plastic bag and then in a larger plastic bag at the bottom of her closet until trash day, she's recently discovered them not wrapped in plastic and in her dresser, under clean sweaters and slips and bras.

Searching for things, opening and closing drawers, going through old purses or envelopes is becoming common practice for Lena. Charlie's also been rummaging through her dresser lately, something he's never done before–doesn't make sense to Lena, but things not making

<96>

sense is becoming more the rule than the exception. It takes a while, but she changes her underpants and this time remembers to wrap the damp ones in a plastic bag.

Carrying her book from her bedroom through the kitchen into the living room, she hears but doesn't understand what Charlie and Rochelle are saying; unless someone is talking directly to her, most conversations meld with crashing silverware, pots and pans, dishes, doorbells, and the occasional train whistle from her hearing aid. She smiles and totters through the kitchen, one hand clutching a Belva Plain novel, the other clutching woodwork and counters and chair backs.

"All the talking!" She pauses for a moment.

"Hi, Grandma." Rochelle flashes her a quick smile.

"I slept through my whole movie, but it's a long time before I fall asleep at night. I have a lot of rosaries to say before I fall asleep. You think I'm asleep, but sometimes it takes hours for me to say all my prayers." Lena rambles on as she continues her trek into the living room.

In what's become known as Grandma's easy chair–next to the fireplace and facing a row of windows along the front of the house–she carefully lowers herself then flops the last few inches into the overstuffed cushions. The Schnoodle sits next to the ottoman on which Lena, no matter how swollen her ankles, never rests her feet. Not ladylike.

"What do you want?" she asks the dog. By nature, she's not an animal person, but after all, she does drop a lot of food. Once Lena puts on her glasses and opens her book, the Schnoodle sulks back into the kitchen, and Lena rereads, enjoying what's familiar and perplexed by what's not.

She's asleep when Charlie calls her from the kitchen for supper–her book on the floor, some of its loose pages strewn across the carpet, and Lena's glasses lopsided across her face.

Charlie finds Lena bending over the stray pages. "I'll get that, Ma. I told you not to pick things up. That's how you fall."

Some months ago, after yanking open the refrigerator door, Lena fell over backwards and banged her head on the

<97>

hardwood floor. Staring up at the kitchen ceiling, she thought of death, how simple it would have been: quick, painless. She scooted herself along on her bottom, closed the refrigerator, and continued into her bedroom, where she sat on the carpet with her back against her bed until Charlie came home from work.

Charlie calls Rochelle several times before she finally comes down from her bedroom to join them for supper.

Lena picks up snippets of Charlie and Rochelle's conversation–something about computers and homework and play rehearsal and eat your broccoli.

"Michael's still working the evening shift?" Lena asks.

"Yes." Charlie faces Lena.

"Hopefully he's not going to work another double," Rochelle adds, but all Lena understands is double, so she fills in the rest.

"Nursing is a hard job," Lena says.

"Not to mention disgusting." Rochelle makes a face to match her comment, and Lena smiles at her granddaughter even though she's not sure why Rochelle is making such a horrible face or what's disgusting. Maybe the chicken is too dry.

"You're such a pretty girl and you stay so slim," Lena says to her granddaughter.

"And smart, too," Charlie adds. "Don't forget the trophy she won for best delegate at the MUN conference last weekend."

Lena doesn't remember the trophy, nor does she know what MUN is, but she's become an expert at improvising. "Who knew that we'd have such a genius in our family?"

Conversation resumes between Charlie and Rochelle, and Lena takes in bits of food along with fragments of conversation and banter, but topics shift too quickly for her to keep up.

Rochelle jumps up from the table, scrapes her plate into the trash, and drops it next to the sink. Then she disappears from the kitchen. Next, Charlie stands and carries his plate to the sink and sets it on top of Rochelle's. "Take your time, Ma. I'll be back down in a few minutes."

Off the Rocks

<98>

Lena remains at the table, the Schnoodle sprawled out next to her, its eyes following Lena's fork.

Charlie's in his bed staring at the news on television—something about Iraq or Afghanistan or Iran. His thoughts are on Michael and how their relationship is like a Chinese painting: more blank space than detail. Why did he doubt that Michael worked a double shift? Why the sudden show of affection and passion this morning when they hadn't had sex in weeks—guilt or some leftover sexual tension from a night of cruising? When Michael found Charlie and Lena in the kitchen this morning, he asked Charlie, "Got a minute?" But later on he never mentioned what it was he wanted to talk about. After sex, Michael fell asleep. Hours later, he awoke, dressed, grabbed a bite to eat, and left for work before Rochelle came home from school. Maybe "Got a minute?" was code for "I'm horny." Or maybe it turned out to be the wrong time to tell Charlie that they were through.

They first met when Charlie volunteered with a local AIDS organization and Michael was a nurse on the floor Charlie frequented. Seems like they've always been care-takers, but somewhere along the way they forgot how to take care of each other, and Charlie wonders if this happened gradually, like erosion over time, or if this fault were always there but suddenly shifted. Regardless, caring for a 13-year-old and a 98-year-old under the same roof is all he can handle for now and he guesses the same is true for Michael.

Maybe it's too much for Michael, but Charlie can't worry about that tonight. He presses the power button on the remote, turns off the light, rolls onto his side, and struggles to empty his mind. Some hours later his bladder calls, and Michael is asleep next to him. No double shift, at least not tonight.

Watching his stream turn the toilet water yellow, he thinks of long-ago Sunday drives in his father's old black Buick, out on Long Island or up to the Catskills, where he'd sit fidgeting in pain until Lena urged Frank to pull over and Charlie would relieve himself alongside the car, often

<99>

peeing on the whitewalls–small revenge for a kid who hated those pointless drives.

He tiptoes down the stairs to check on his mother and recalls a particularly unpleasant car trip through a tidy Long Island development where all the houses and automobiles and people and dogs looked alike. Cloned children played on cloned front lawns: boys, catch or basketball; girls, jump rope or hopscotch.

"See, Frank?" Lena said. "If we lived in a neighborhood like this one, Charlie would have more friends his age."

"What difference would it make?" Frank pointed his chin toward the car window. "He'd still be over there playing with the girls."

"That's not true, Frank," Lena retorted. In the rearview mirror, Charlie caught his mother's pained expression.

He opens the French doors to his mother's room and remembers another time–he was about Rochelle's age–when it was his mother who said, "If I had a child who was a homosexual, I'd rather he be dead."

Lena's head lifts as he opens the door. She holds up her right hand and crystal rosaries dangle from her fingers. Charlie enters the room, dimly lit from a small lamp on an ornate, gold-painted desk, and he leans in closely over Lena's bed. "Are you okay, Ma?"

Lena nods and Charlie kisses her forehead. She takes her son's hand. "Thank you, Charlie. For everything."

Before returning to his own bed, he checks on Rochelle. She's asleep, the dog curled up at her feet.

As Charlie climbs back into bed, Michael stirs and asks if everything is okay. "Everything's fine," Charlie answers.

Drifting, he's in a summer bungalow in the legendary South Beach–his only visit to the area, though he's heard many South Beach stories. He watches fireflies through screened windows and doors as his mother sits at an enamel-top kitchen table, sipping coffee and inching a plate of homemade doughnuts toward Charlie. He's about nine-years-old, and a boy, maybe five years older, carrying a six-pack of empty soda bottles, opens the screen door. The door slams and the bottles clink. "Any empties?" the boy asks, and he grabs a doughnut from the plate. His dirty

<100>

blond hair is slicked back except for the curls forming a V
on his forehead, and his t-shirt sleeves are rolled up above
his tanned shoulders, and he walks with a slight swagger.
Charlie falls asleep trying to recall the boy's name.

Lena dreams of the long-ago, rambling summerhouse in
South Beach with the wide, screened-in porch and
cascading hydrangeas. Its kitchen is a wash of sunlight,
and curtains sway on ocean breezes to the songs of seagulls
and children as Lena takes a tray of cookies from the oven,
sets the tray on a well-worn butcher block, then throws off
her oven mitts and searches for the spatula. Charlie and
Michael and Rochelle appear, glowing and windblown and
salted from the beach.
"Hi, Grandma!" Rochelle smiles her beautiful smile.
"Look at what I baked for you while you three were off
swimming," Lena says, lifting the tray of cookies.
"They look delicious, Grandma. You're the best!"
Rochelle hugs Lena and gives her a big kiss.

Martin Altman

Stranger

I, a woman estranged by the man I am,
Seek shelter in the forest.
As a silent flower, rain-soaked, sighs,
I befriend the spy.
I stare at the invisible icon of goddess,
A face decayed of lush leaves.
From end to end
Her torn, moist mouth
Breathes into mine.
The flaming forest in her eyes,
I forgot to cry.

<102>

<103>

Chelsey Clammer

Pounce

I do not know how to approach my desire, my want to push this friendship into something more. My flirting, like my writing, needs a prompt, a nudge. But there is nothing here to shove me forward but the sight of her body. Her body, which actually gives no sign that my friend feels the same. There are no indicators that there is another narrative going on besides the one of our friendship. And yet I want something more. I want to dive into the story of her body, want to feel my teeth sink into the words of her skin. I want to turn the page, to feel the laughs of a friend bend into the gasps of a lover. But I do not know how to pounce, how to introduce this topic, how to bring our bodies into a different sort of conversation, how to tell my friend I want something more, how to stretch out my lips, encourage her to slide closer to me, to slip from the topic of friend to one of lover.

She has short brown hair. Dark eyebrows curve around her large brown eyes. Between them, a patch of smooth, plucked skin is exposed. It is a wide plane of skin I want to touch, rub. Like the soft spot on a dog's forehead, or a lover's. But she is not a lover, just a friend. A friend I met only six months ago, and saw for only two days back then.

We were on a lake, at an impromptu writing retreat made with two other friends. She arrived at the beach house with a book in one hand and a blue duffel bag slung over her bare shoulder. Her black tank top revealed arms decorated with tattoos of her favorite lines of poetry. She is a work of art. After she put her things away, she emerged from the sliding glass doors and stretched out her body on the warm summer sand. The sun radiated onto her, bounced back into my eyes. She shielded her own eyes with a book on feminist theory, laid the pages across her face, the spine and cover soaked in the sun. As she napped, I

<104>

took in the sight of her, her body, and thought of what I would like to do with that body. Instant attraction.

When she finally woke from her nap, she joined me on the porch and we lost ourselves in a conversation that felt as if we had always been two friends talking. Instant connection.

With her words, she became more than just a body, but a friend. Our dialogue wasn't one in which we introduced ourselves, but one in which we sank into the topics of life, as if we had always been talking like this, had always been friends. We immediately melded into each other's lives, and I fell for her energy, those eyes. Instant confusion.

I saw her as a new friend, but fell hard for her like you do with a new crush. I felt something for her mind, felt more for her body, felt confused as I tried to figure out which I wanted: friend or lover. What I knew is that I wanted her, this new person in my life, to be something, to mean something to me. I wondered if in the next two days I would gather the courage to enter her room at night.

I never did, and so she is just a friend.

I find myself in this situation again, where I want my friend to be my lover, my lover to always be my friend. I want conversations to include kisses, sex to include a deep knowing like only a friend can know, can understand. Such brain space this consumes, this constant wondering if a friend could be, should be more. I want to say, "The last time this happened..." But it's always happening, still happening.

Six months after our initial meeting at the lake, she sits in Minneapolis on the brown couch across from me. Her feet are planted assuredly, comfortably on the hardwood floor. The winter whirls around outside of my apartment. She has driven up from Texas to visit for a few days, come during her Winter Break from grad school to see the friend she considers me to be. We wrote sporadic correspondences while she was in school: e-mails sent in early morning hours, carving out the space to let our friendship grow through words.

Now, in front of me, her body finally sharing space with mine, her attitude is one of ease and engagement. She asks

<105>

me questions about my family, and I backtrack to the important parts, weave a tale that tells where I'm at with them now, tells a little bit more about myself. It is a long story, an extensive answer, and she stays with it, wide-eyed and intrigued the whole time. She thinks I'm interesting, smart. She has read my e-mails, my words, my essays, and thinks they are astoundingly well-crafted. I love her a little bit more for this.

I consider compliments about my writing a subtle flirtation style, a way to gain my confidence that something more could happen, should happen. Stroke my ego and there's much more I will want for you to touch. But I am not that forward, not that capable of showing you what it is I want. Think I am brilliant and I will blush, become shy. I'll want you to, will wait for you to pull me out of myself, draw me into a new breath. It is interesting that I only allow my friends to read my essays. Perhaps I set myself up. Perhaps. I hold my breath. I wait.

It is her first morning here, the morning after the night in which we talked for hours, the night in which I ultimately declared I must go to sleep because I was too shy to take our bodies elsewhere, to persuade us from our friendly conversation to bodies slippery with sweat, sticky with sex. She is only in town for two days. The countdown has begun. And now I am awake. I sit in the living room at 4am, writing. I sit in the same chair in which I sat last night. My knees, as they were last night, are curled toward my chest, keeping me from, hiding me from what it is I want to do. Now, as I write these things about her eyebrows and the way she sat confidently across from me last night, she sleeps deeply down the hall. I wish I could hear her breathing, to feel a part of her existence sitting in this room with me.

The last time this happened, when I actually turned a friend into a lover, I lost the friend, lost the lover. Our connection grew too intense, too full of our energies, and we had to eventually drift away from each other, to let our connection die down, to desensitize itself, to hibernate with the thought, the hope that it would emerge again.

It didn't. We are no longer lovers, our friendship is lost.

<106>

This is what I risk.

Outside, it is snowing. And in the white swirls that coat the outside world, a steady silence has taken over. Inside, we, too, are silent. It is a week past Christmas, but the tree is still up; the twinkling white lights illuminate my constantly moving pen. The sound of this blue pen scratching fills the air as she rests heavily, silently in the bed down the hall. I feel my body wanting to move toward it, to drift down the corridor, and slither under her sheets. I wonder at how she would respond to this, if she would shift her body toward mine, if we would break the silence.

The last time this almost happened, and I say "almost happened" because I couldn't muster the courage to pounce, I found myself syncing my life in tune with hers so we would always be near each other. I held back so I could dive further into the friendship. By not pursuing the possibility of a lover, I became more confident in asking for "friendly" physical contact. Frequent hugs, kisses on the cheek, back rubs to ease her stress, cuddling when I felt sad. I touched her body many times, but her body was never mine to touch. We are good friends now. I doubt we will ever be lovers. And yet, I still find myself waiting, wondering, wanting more.

She continues to sleep in the bed, and I think about how this is the third time this has happened in three years, the third friend I have wished to become something else. I call her a friend, I know her as such, and yet... She moved to Texas for school, I stayed in Minneapolis waiting for her holiday break, waiting to see what would happen when she came back, thinking this time I would say something, would make my move, would pounce. She is down the hall. I am in the chair. My mind is down the hall with her, on top of her body. The snow has picked up again, has created a curtain between us and the world. We are secluded, tucked into my apartment. I will imagine what the day could be like, fantasize that we will stay inside with the reasoning that the weather is too treacherous to face. Excuses to keep us excluded from the world, to keep our bodies warm with each other.

Off the Rocks

<107>

At 5am I will stop imagining, stop writing. I will set my pen down and I will make my decision. I will put down my notebook and return to a bed, one of the two beds in this apartment. I will travel the length of the hallway, look at my door, look at hers. I will move. I will stand in a doorway, mustering up some version of confidence to proceed, either back to my life as a friend or into a new one we could consider ours. A shared one, one full of swirling bodies. I will rest my head on the chosen doorframe, steady my body with both hands. I will gaze up at the bed, wonder if this is the time, the right bed into which I will slither. I will let out a sigh, still uncertain, as I step closer to a mattress. I will cross the threshold. The floorboards will creak under my weight, as I weigh out the consequences of my decision. Outside, the snow will gain speed, will pour down from the morning white sky.

It was not her room into which I entered last night. Instead, I lay down in my own bed, my thoughts continuing to hover over her body. I fell back asleep, had a dream full of kisses. In the dream, her lips felt like plastic, soft yet firm, allowing me to bend into them just so. Now, it is four hours past that dream, four hours since she woke up, and we continue our friendly discussion as the sun starts to break into the day. We enter into the world, do not exclude ourselves from the cold. We take in the crisp air and talk with mouths full of excited breath while we traverse the city, braving the weather, weaving in and out of coffee shops and bookstores throughout the day. We forget our desire to write, and fall into each other's mouths, sentences, breath. I still want to fall onto her tongue.

I have tripped into many mouths before, crossed the threshold of friendly conversation into tongues thick with desire. The women who started out as friends, then gained speed as we danced into lovers. Their bodies guided mine, knew my body deeper than I know it myself. They have tasted my sweat, read the words of my skin as I laid them down, naked before their eyes, allowing myself to be well-read. We let ourselves slip into something deeper. It has rarely turned out well. It has, in fact, never lasted longer

<108>

than a few months. The lovers have always receded back into friends, if not dissolved altogether. But the ones who stuck around, the ones who could take the twists and curves of a relationship that grew then receded into something else, the thing we originally knew, are the ones in my life who know me well, know me as a lover, know me as a friend. A perfect knowing.

She sits across from me again. I have given her my words to read, an essay I wrote on sex and masturbation. My mode of flirtation. The essay is not about her, and yet I hope to draw her in with my words. She cracks up, laughing at the awkward and often hilarious sexual situations I have survived. Her fair cheeks blush, her fingers cover the exposed teeth of her smile. I can taste her chortles, and want to feel them vibrate underneath my skin. I want those teeth to bite my ear, want to feel her body surround mine, to know of her inside of me. Want the friend to fuck me. She continues to read.

A year before this there was another friend, another desire for a lover. I had just started writing with her, and she, the more seasoned writer, sent me essays she was working on for me to read. They were all about sex and desire. I didn't know her that well, had only known her for a month, actually, and I started to consider her words to be flirtation devices. But we were just friends, freshly emerging from the status of acquaintances. She sent me essay after essay, six in total, all about sex, desire, lesbian relationships, and heat. I continued to read these as signs of flirtation. The thought consumed me, her essays consumed all of my reading time, all of my spare time, all of my time. And yet our friendship was still forming. And yet...

I called her one day, shortly after we had written together, and I asked her flat out, because I wanted to—needed to—know, "Are we flirting or becoming friends?"

A brave question.

One I find myself wanting to ask now.

The sun breaks through the clouds of snow. Streams of light fall across her face, bounce into my eyes. I am still

<109>

amazed by her visage, the way she presents, exudes her face to the world. Brave. Confident. After more hours of conversation, the sun begins to sigh. I feel sleepy with desire, sleepy with this pressing need for something more. I tell her I need to leave this coffee shop, need to go home to nap. And while it is true that I am slightly tired, there is something else I want to do. Mainly, I want to give myself an opportunity to pounce, to see if when we return home I will offer the idea of a kiss.

We get home. I take a shower just in case she, too, will want to taste the body of a friend. I lie down in my bed; she lies down in my roommate's bed, her resting spot while my roommate is shacked up with her boyfriend across town. I am restless, full of questions I want answered. Mainly, does she feel the same? I wonder if she is awake, if she's just lying there like I am lying here, thinking.

Sleepless, I move my body to the living room, hope the creaking floorboards will mention to her that I am awake. I take my body to the brown couch, and I lie down with my questions. How to broach this topic? How to ask, to state, to do? Do I ask for a kiss? Do I just do? And this is how it feels to want a friend: you want more, but you do not want to ruin.

What I had before with the friend who did turn into a lover but eventually turned into a ruin, was a friend I lost, a thing now gone. Her name was Sam. But before the ruin, there was bliss. We were friends, we were lovers, we were perfect.

A shift. She is napping in the bedroom. The 5pm sunset pinks the creamy walls. I continue to stay on the couch, to try and settle into a nap for lack of anything else to do, try to quiet my body that is screaming for a conversation, a something, a knowing. I can only stay like this for a few seconds, though, cannot stand these questions any longer.

I push myself up out of an urge, a wanting to know. She is only in town for two more days, so I must know before it becomes too late. I must say something, must get the energy and thoughts of her lips that well up inside of me out into the air. I again travel down the length of the

<110>

hallway then brace my hands against the frame of the bedroom door. "Chloe. Are you asleep?" I whisper.

A scene. I whisper across the space of the bed, into Sam's attentive ears, that she is amazing. We are sitting cross-legged on my mattress. Her eyes are shining with something, and I think they are shining with want. Here is my best friend staring hard into my own eyes. Here is my best friend coyly biting her lip.

Chloe rolls over in the bed. I stand at the foot of it, leaning farther into the room. There is not much space between our bodies, but the distance I must travel to get to her feels huge. With my roommate gone, though, there actually is much space for us, much room to explore, much time to ourselves. There is much that could happen. I whisper again, a bit louder, "Are you sleeping?" Her body shifts closer to mine.

I smile back at her, biting my own lip, and scoot my butt a little bit closer to Sam's. Our knees touch. This is my best friend getting closer to me. I smile at the thought. I can feel the heat of her skin radiate through our jeans. I inch forward just a little bit more, and we continue to gaze into each other's eyes as I scoot just a little bit closer.

Chloe shifts her body toward mine. Groggily, she says, "Huh? No, I'm—I'm awake. What's up?"

Here is my chance. I have interrupted her nap for no other reason than to tell her how I feel. I'm unsure of what to say, of how I really feel. So I tell her what I do know. "So, here's the deal," I say, sitting my knees on the mattress near her legs. "I have a crush on you."

I reach out and put my hand on Sam's knee.

Chloe rolls over to me, laughs.

I put my other hand on Sam's other knee. Her face flushes.

Chloe sits up in bed.

Sam grabs my waist with both hands and pulls me closer to her. I sit up on my knees and begin to lean in.

"I have a crush on you, too," Chloe says.

Sam stretches her head forward, her lips begin to pucker.

I laugh, too.

Off the Rocks

<111>

Sam keeps her eyes open, I hold her gaze, and we lean in a bit farther. The inches between us close. I can feel the warmness of her breath on my lips, my lips as they, too, begin to pucker.

"So what do we do about this?" I laugh, question, hope.

<112>

<113>

Andrea Lambert

Generic Butch-Femme Poem

The way you slick your hair to the side
Then ask me to razor the back
The way you pose in your wife-beater
Your breasts bound with an ACE bandage
Pink glitter scraped off your nails

When I met you,
It was bows and bows, and ruffles, glitter,
Curtains of hair down your back.

It was slow, the transformation
And in a way, I changed, too
Camping it up, playing femme a little higher
Blond bouffant, pencil skirt, heels more MILF-y

When all the buzzwords are shed like
Masturbation or petals on a reality TV show
Leaving the bed clear
It's you and I and we're naked
And I fold my arms around you
And you kiss my neck sweetly,
And the curtain closes
        That's all, folks

<114>

<115>

Timothy David Rey

How to Start Being (Gay)

First,
take a deep breath.
You
are going to need it.
And see how far that gets you,
what stops it lets you make
and where
at what
well-worn-down depots.

Memorize their names
as quick as you can
and
as quickly then
forget them.
They are not for you, no, you
are holding out for the scenic view,
for the wanton look
and the settled gaze.
This is how you'll live out your days
If you can just make it past—

Yes, first you'll need a
Real
Big
Breath.
Take it in and see how
good it tastes, the flawless line that
it creates, the perfect,
finite, persuasive
case that
grasps you sure and tight.

<116>

So you'll go beat
the different drum
and sing a song
that's seldom sung
and hear:

The view awaits you, son,
that's how it's done!

But first...

<117>

Ryan M. Mattern

The Skeleton in My Closet

The skeleton in my closet
keeps me up at night with jazz records.
The thin sounds of saxophones
seep underneath my closet door
and dash my dreams against sweat-soaked pillows.

When I yank the door open
to ask the skeleton if he minds,
to remind him it's two in the morning,
he pushes his brown bowler derby
up and out of his black eye sockets
with a long, bony finger.
Don't be a square, daddy-O! he says,
then continues to play drums
with metal coat hangers,
tapping along to "The Shadow of Your Smile."

The skeleton in my closet
does not respect houseguests.
When my neighbors come over
to play rummy, he sings over Miles,
Ain't you folks got nothin' to do
on a Sat-a-day night?
They comment on the peat notes
of my Glenfiddich.
Politely, they pretend not
to hear him.

The skeleton comes out of the closet
when I share my bed with women.
I steal his Thelonious Monk record
and melt the wax of sweet-smelling candles

<118>

while they lie in bed, considering the light
underneath my closet door.
When they close their eyes
and their breath becomes labored,
rapt in the pulsing of our bodies,
the skeleton rips the needle off the record
and climbs into bed with us.
He looks me in the eyes,
reminds me he is here.

<119>

Walter Beck

National Coming Out Day 2011

For the first time
I didn't avoid the question
Would you like your picture taken?

Ten months ago
I burned down a cage
Of eight years,
Smashed and burned
The closet down
And lit my cigarette
On the smoldering embers.

No, I didn't avoid the question,
Held a sign high and proud:
Bisexual
In my rainbow bracelets
And black beret,
Battered jeans
And my Eyehategod shirt.

Ten months
And a long walk since
Always waiting for the other shoe
To drop,
To flush years of work
Down.

She snapped the picture
With my rock 'n' roll grin,
Headphones barking out
Jon Ginoli's "Anthem."

<120>

Am I committing career suicide
With one snap of a camera?
Other brothers and sisters
Who've served with me
Still in their own private hells,
Afraid to lose it all.

I gave her my e-mail
To send me a copy of the picture
So I could show it
To the whole damn world.

Looking out that charred door—
Liberty?
Freedom?
Destruction?

The law still commands me to be brave.

<121>

H.L. Sudler

Yesterdays and Tomorrows

What have you learned from your life? What will you take with you when you die? Will it be all the lessons you have learned, all the pain you remember? Romances, milestones, regrets, eras?

Somehow I always manage to return in my head to the events that have hallmarked my life, steering it into a direction unforeseen, jarring me out of complacency or ignorance; an existence created as if I lived on a whole other plane than the rest of the world. I turn these thoughts over like pancakes on a griddle, flipping events this way and that, examining them, but always arriving at the same questions for which I have no absolute answer.

What have you learned from your life? What will you take with you when you die?

I ask myself these questions on my birthday, as I always ask myself these questions at what I believe to be the most reflective time of year. Since that date comes around in December, the same month as World AIDS Day, I always have cause to remember the three men I had come to know in my life, all at the same time, dead from AIDS—dead and buried, gone from the world, gone before I even knew they had the disease, gone, it seems, even from collective memory.

Lawrence Blakely, Laurence Gray, and Bernard Little were all friends of mine in high school—and let them be remembered here and now, for they are all forgotten. We spent three years together laughing, joking, studying, creating memories, but also growing as kids do, foraging into adulthood as if with blindfolds donned and hands outstretched. We held on to each other, relied on each other, fought and made up, not realizing the importance of

<122>

our friendship, not realizing the importance of our bond as men, as African-American men, as gay African-American men.

Laurence Gray was my girlfriend's sidekick at that time. He was very short and lively with a wide, infectious smile and an equally contagious laugh. His face beamed and lit up a room, but he was also very emotional and would cry at the drop of a hat. He lived a terrible life at home—his family was poor and he was often hungry and no one wanted him. He became one of my best friends, as he was always at my girlfriend's side, keeping her laughing, keeping her company. I was dour and very serious then, as I am now, but he had the natural ability to make anyone laugh, even me.

He was partially responsible for me winning a student government campaign—handing out flyers and making up posters. I helped him with his studies, shared my lunch with him or gave him money to keep him fed during the day. We held a Secret Santa for our group of friends one Christmas and I remember him gifting my girlfriend a white stuffed bear that she adored. I remember him in a fight once, and I remember being shocked at how strong he was for a little guy, how much anger he carried with him. He was proud to be an Aquarius.

Bernard was a little taller. Make that a lot. Taller than my five feet seven inches. But he was lanky and not terribly good-looking. If he had been given the opportunity to grow older, he might have grown into his looks and become handsome. Either way, he was a busybody, and what old timers would call "a hoot." He referred to himself as Millie and he would breeze through the school hallways, his lunch in a wrinkled plastic supermarket bag dangling from his wrist, his torn schoolbag held together by safety pins, his outfits shit brown and polyester, worn sometimes two or three times a week, smelling stale. He had grown up disadvantaged and pushed on his grandmother. You could tell in his eyes that he sensed his future had limited options and that he was living only for today.

He gravitated toward me like a dedicated puppy dog and we developed a strange friendship. He loved my bad boy

<123>

attitude, that I was fearless, tough, and direct. He was a confidant, even though we never discussed our common sexuality. Like me, he was a member of the school's drama club, and on breaks we would joke around and he would laugh gaily and without conscience. Everyone knew him: teachers, staff, nerds, jocks. Out of school he was considered a nobody, invisible. But in school he was a celebrity in our little high school soap opera; comic relief that reminded us that if someone like him could find laughter despite his circumstances, so could the rest of us. So we embraced him as much as we could.

Lawrence Blakely was a radically different story altogether. He was in each of my classes but he and I were not all that close. He was tall, husky, black as newly applied tar and just as shiny. Yet, for as large as he was, he walked with dainty little steps, like a girl, as if he were worried he would disturb the universe with his presence. He spoke in a small, nasally voice, his eyes distorted behind unflattering bifocals. His teeth were unnaturally white, and from time to time he emitted a laughter that was deep and throaty, as if to hint at the man he would become.

A week before our senior graduation, Lawrence Blakely and Laurence Gray got into a fight in the chemistry lab—an epic battle not unlike David and Goliath. I was the school's student government vice-president at that time and, knowing the fight could prevent them from participating in commencement ceremonies, tried to break them up. It turned out to be a huge mistake. The massive Lawrence Blakely attacked me and all three of us found ourselves in the principal's office with the threat of suspension over our heads.

Then there was graduation. Then they were dead.

After we left high school, I never saw or heard from Lawrence Blakely or Laurence Gray ever again, and saw Bernard Little only once. As I was walking down the street in downtown Philadelphia one day about five years after graduation, another friend from school (who was also black and gay) informed me that Bernard Little and Laurence Gray had died within a week of each other. The funerals had been two and three weeks prior. A little more than a

<124>

year later, this same friend would tell me of Lawrence Blakely's death. Despite the fact that he had lost weight, shed his glasses and his timid gait, and became a gym boy—fully evolved into the butterfly he was meant to be—he, too, succumbed quickly to the disease. All of their families had disowned them and they suffered and died for the most part alone.

I was so burned by this, so ashamed that I had immersed myself in college life and parties, that I was spurred to do something in their memory. I would not allow these men to rest in my brain as nothing more than fading tombstones in a cemetery. I began to volunteer at local Philadelphia AIDS charities: ActionAIDS and From All Walks of Life, MANNA and SafeGuards, doing everything from selling pies to handing out condoms and literature at clubs. I attended fundraisers, volunteered at AIDS walks and LGBT Pride festivals. I served as a Buddy to people suffering from HIV and AIDS and a mentor to others looking to serve.

The people I encountered at these organizations changed my life. They were angels, amazing one and all, each of them so different from the other, yet all of them bound together in grief and hope. My favorites were 67-year-old Mister Jim, who volunteered in the memory of his beloved son; and the rough and tough Jimmy O., as young and handsome as he was, was a man who never got over losing the love of his life, whose grief cloaked him like a scent, who volunteered courageously and, seemingly, tirelessly. The soldiers at these organizations were like a secret society working diligently for people they had lost, and for people they knew were suffering from the disease, for people they did not know at all: men, women, gay, straight, transgendered, young, old, Black, White, Latino, Asian. The hours were long and there was always so much to do, but we existed as a family unto ourselves and they welcomed me with open arms.

I was ashamed of my ignorance—for that is the only word that aptly describes my situation. How dare I shield myself from this truth as prevalent as it was in its first two decades, that which had such impact on my community!

<125>

How dare I believe that it could not affect my circle! That I was buffered; AIDS reduced down, chalked up, to a head-line, a broadcast, something that people who were not like me suffered, something that people who were careless or uninformed suffered. Today I would like to think that if I had known about Lawrence, Laurence, and Bernard, I would have come running in the pouring rain to stand beside them in their final hours. I did not even think to check on them after graduation, to inquire after them, my blood brothers, during a crisis that I knew was striking down lives indiscriminately.

This brings me to the prevalent arrogance and ignorance that exists at a national level, where the number of deaths and infections are still rising, and affecting demographics worldwide. Where apprehensions about an open, honest dialogue on sex and sexuality still prevent us from saving lives. Where, despite the fact that there is so much money spent on preventative measures for other health issues, not enough is designated to this disease or reaches the people truly in need: the financially disadvantaged, the uninsured and under-insured, the young, the uneducated.

What have you learned from your life? What will you take with you when you die?

I remember my friend Ted Kirk, whom I helped to take care of up until his dying day. I remember his wispy blond hair, his smiling eyes, and broad laugh. I remember feeding him his dinner when he could no longer feed himself. I remember helping him bathe and use the bathroom and getting him in and out of bed. I remember sitting with him for long stretches in the evenings as we watched *Law & Order*, one of his favorite television shows. I remember when he had to be moved to a hospice, and the people there who were so pleasant and worked so tirelessly. I remember him marrying his boyfriend from a wheelchair, his dementia, and the times when I thought he would not make it through another night; then finally his quiet death, like a light summer breeze that enters a room and just as effortlessly exits.

When I die I am determined to leave behind my ignorance, for Earth is the only place where it belongs. I

<126>

shall leave behind my regrets as well, becoming weightless and free. What is past has passed. I will take with me only my memories of loves, lovers, and friends; of sunny, golden days long gone. And of the work I have done here on Earth and the people I have met. I will also take with me the days of Lawrence and Laurence and Bernard. I will cherish our fun together as children in the face of life's harsh realities, our laughter, our finite number of memories. And of the lessons they taught me, which I will forever hold dear to my heart.

<127>

Daniel W.K. Lee

First Aid

for C. Lopez

If I slash my ring-fingertip w/an X-Acto knife:
against OSHA regulations, you should tenderly
risk your lips, knead the red edges together.

<128>

Off the Rocks

<129>

Marty McConnell

Strength Starts the "It Gets Moderately More Tolerable" Campaign

Don't say it's too hard, the world.
but also do not say it gets better
just because we survive it. Oh,

these wings, these albatross portions
strapped to our backs. Let us not belittle

our suffering by saying it's behind us.
Each day a man wakes up loving a man
is a day at war. Make no mistake: things

are better, somewhere. For some of us.
The woman who has her own talk show

is hilarious. And a cosmetics spokesmodel
in flat shoes. But the spread on her wedding
in *People Magazine* included not one kiss

between the brides. I am allowed
to be bothered by this. To look

at my lover on the subway and think: if you
were in the hospital, could I pass for your sister
and receive permission to spend the night

watching you breathe? Beautiful boys, do not
jump off of bridges or wind ropes

around your evolutionary
throats. We are failing you
as slowly as we can.

<130>

Sarah Fonseca

For Tyler Clementi

You'd been captured,
Captioned,
Standing on the second-highest stage
Of your life,
Horsehair bow drawn,
A weapon against
The well-hidden demon
Who waged its war against you
In dark bars
In bedrooms with thin walls

Poised, submissive
You waited
For the conductor's baton to dictate
Accents, crescendos, and
The speed of blood coursing
Through your ripe, translucent
Body
You waited
For the downbeat that would drown
Your tormentors' concerto

I stared at you, the newsprint boy,
Still waiting for your music,
The demure sounds of a violin solo
Now frozen stiff by the Hudson
I was too many hours away in distance
I was too many hours away in time

Your highest stage was on those railings,
Every ear—
The deaf
The busy

<132>

The intolerant—
Took in that pained wail
When the bow of your body
Fired across your thinning heartstrings
And the splash, as your ripples in the water
Gave way
To powerful waves of sound

<133>

Dario Dalla Lasta

Livin' on a Prayer

When I was bullied in junior high and high school, there was no one to talk to.

There were no resources to take advantage of, and no television shows existed that brought our plight to life. Guidance counselors were scarce and unusual. If you were sent to one, that meant you had a drug problem or were going to be expelled. There was no such thing as going online (privately or with a best friend) to check out gay teen suicide prevention hotlines. It was hard enough to look at dirty books in the library, let alone whisper to a stodgy librarian: "Uh, can you help me find a program that can help sissy boys like me?" A blank stare is all you would receive in return, if you even dared to ask.

And being reared on the wholesome *Brady Bunch* children, who had no real problems except sibling rivalry and a swollen nose, was quite unlike the current television hit *Glee* with its out-of-the-closet, well-adjusted, show tunes-singin', Lady Gaga-lovin' high school kids surrounded by understanding and accepting adults.

Back in the late 1970's and early 1980's, you were on your own.

Bullying in schools has become a hot-button topic of the day and for that, I am grateful. Thirty years ago, being mercilessly picked on was just an everyday occurrence that you had to endure to get through seven school periods of hell. I wish there had been a concerted effort back then on the part of parents, teachers, and administrators to look at the problem, acknowledge it, and take steps to alleviate it. I wish I had spoken up and asked for help. But they didn't tackle the issue, and I didn't tell anyone what was happening. The subject was both taboo and nonexistent.

Did bullying lead me into suicidal despair? Yes. A lot. Did it make me feel like shit, like a nobody, like a stupid

<134>

little girly faggot? Uh huh. And yet, I didn't kill myself or harm myself in any way. Looking back, I'm surprised—there I awkwardly stood: an innocent, trusting, naïve, and sexually confused boy who had no survival skills, backbone, or street smarts. A sweet child with long hair and effeminate mannerisms, I was completely unaware of how threatening I was to boys exploding into puberty. But soon enough, their wrath and hatred for me and what I was became apparent. Instead of folding into nothingness, however, I learned to cope in an intolerant society, to toughen up, to become the man that I am today. And for that, I am also grateful. I'm definitely one of the lucky ones.

While I didn't flourish into a blooming flower of ravishing beauty (like I dreamed of being), my evolution took a different course, as I transformed into something more akin to a weed or a spot of crabgrass; still a part of plant life, but unwanted and always picked last. Although ridiculed as being nothing more than that thin and rejected reed, I found I could be trampled but not broken, able to remain resilient under the heel of a haughty boot.

The story begins in a white, middle-class, suburban neighborhood of Sacramento, California, where I played outside with neighbors way past dark, walked to and from school without accompaniment, made up dance routines with my older sister, and believed that Jesus died for my sins. And while I am not religious anymore, I think that my boyhood faith saved my skinny ass. I've been thinking long and hard about why I didn't end it all back in 1978 or 1980, why I survived, and why I didn't hang myself from a tree in the backyard or drown myself in Mrs. Mitchell's pool next door. And the answer has been eluding me for years.

Over and over again, I asked myself: what in the world did I do, what did I have that others don't have now? And then suddenly it hit me while reading the latest news story about another teenage boy from a small town who was gay, bullied, and led down the tortured path to suicide.

As hard as it may be to personally fathom, I believe my salvation boils down to this: I grew up with religion, with a spiritual path and a firm commitment to a Higher Power.

<135>

Believing in God and praying to my Heavenly Father instead of my mortal one pulled me out of the depths of depression time and time again and allowed me to find something transcendent, something beyond me and my pitiful world of spitballs and name-calling and physical intimidation. I think prayer saved my life.

Now I'm not saying that I agree with organized religion or that I'm staunchly Catholic or Protestant or Lutheran or attached to any church typical of my childhood demographic. Far from it. To be honest, I haven't stepped inside a church on my own accord for years except for the occasional wedding or baptism. The thought makes me shudder. What would I even do at a church service these days? Roll my eyes? Fall to the floor in a paroxysm of fervent confession? Burn in hell? I honestly don't know.

All I do know is that having a power bigger than myself, a loving figurehead to unburden all my horror stories to in private without being judged, delivered me from death as a youngster struggling to make his feeble way in the world. Whether I had been saved by the blood of Christ during communion or by allowing Jesus into my heart at a Christian youth camp, the details didn't matter. The fact was that I had something—no, *Someone*—to talk to anytime, anywhere, a benevolent force that comforted me when I was in trouble and needed help.

I sang along fervently to the inspiring records of Keith Green and Amy Grant and 2nd Chapter of Acts long before I turned to Nirvana. Those albums created a musical path for me to work through my incessant troubles and "give it up to the Lord." Although such a proclamation sounds cheesy now, I honestly believe that if I hadn't been able to do that with my problems, I would have taken them to my grave.

Flash forward 30 years or so. Nowadays, I'm worried that the majority of kids don't have the basic necessity of faith in their lives; instead they have Sony PlayStations, Internet porn, iPhones, and American Express cards. But those things aren't enough to get through the tough and confusing times of adolescence. Like the poor kids who are spoken of in sad, hushed tones on the news and all over the

<136>

Web, I've also been bullied, scorned, ridiculed, teased, smacked, and taunted. Just like Jesus Christ. That's what I believed growing up, and that's what got me through my trials and tribulations.

Huh. Maybe I am just a big old Jesus freak after all.

But I wonder: would He accept a tattooed gay man who recently married his male soul mate while living a fabulously hedonistic lifestyle in New York? I think so. I certainly hope so. Because where would we all be in this world without hope? I'd be dead, another casualty buried and forgotten in the war of growing up gay.

I wish I could tell these children that they can have more, that there even is more. It's hard to believe in that when you're so young and you don't even know yourself yet. I certainly didn't. It took years of growing up—painfully—to do so, but I've finally found myself at a place in my life where I've become exactly who I've always wanted to be. Or, more importantly, who I'm meant to be. And that process took a lot of struggle and heartbreak and hard lessons. The road ain't easy, but it's terribly rewarding.

These boys who are picked on so mercilessly need the opportunity to go down that path, too, in order to reach their full potential. They need the chance to grow up and find that out for themselves. Hell, it took me over 40 years, but I finally did it, and now I'm so happy, I'm delirious.

This is my message for those young kids out there: sure, it gets better, but in the meantime, you can pray. There is something bigger and better than those stupid assholes who find their only strength in bullying those smaller and different and nicer than them. There is Someone who will always listen. Whatever and whoever you believe in, whether it be Jesus or Allah or Buddha or Krishna or Jehovah or Yahweh, it can help to pray and can inspire hope in your heart. "Hope springs eternal in the human breast; Man never Is, but always To be blest: The soul, uneasy and confin'd from home, Rests and expatiates in a life to come." A poet named Alexander Pope wrote that back in 1733, part of his epic "An Essay on Man." Those are some simple yet effective words.

<137>

I hope the boys and girls growing up today amidst the confusion of nonstop information, of both real and virtual harassment, don't give up. There is hope! Not only does it get better; it gets amazingly unbelievable when you follow your heart and do what you love. Again, I'm not religious. I hardly pray anymore myself, and I'm certainly no preacher. I'm barely even a writer. But I'm more than just that flower I always hoped I'd blossom into; now I'm an entire floral arrangement filled with more colors and combinations and complexities than I ever thought possible, especially as a young boy with feathered hair and knobby knees and a high voice in middle school.

I just wish I knew what those young people were missing in order to push them through their tough times. Being a teenager sucks—it always has and it always will—but at least I had church choir and Young Life, doting parents and a loving sister, my own personal relationship with a God I called my own who was bigger and stronger than me, and a powerful, ebullient hope that shone through the agonies I endured on behalf of school bullies in order to stay alive.

In the hallowed words of Bon Jovi, guess you could say I was livin' on a prayer.

<139>

Allison Fradkin

Thanking My Lucky Star

I just think of you and I start to glow.
"Lucky Star"

Madonna may not be the most punctual person in the
world (her concerts are great, just be prepared to wait), but
the woman has impeccable timing. Madonna came into my
life in 1998 when I was 14 and about to enter high school,
otherwise known as the abyss of adolescence. I'd been
watching *A League of Their Own* a lot that summer, and
my favorite part was always the end. Once the credits
started rolling, the song started playing. You know the
one—"This Used to Be My Playground." It isn't included on
the soundtrack, so I had to buy Madonna's CD *Something
to Remember*. Then I had to buy Madonna's CD *Like a
Virgin*. And *Like a Prayer*. And *True Blue*. And *Madonna*,
of course. And then I bought... Well, let's just say that by
the time I started school that fall, I had amassed an
immaculate collection.

*Everybody wants to shine... But it's got to come from
inside... Don't be afraid to fall. I'll hear you when you call
and I'll be right here by your side. Don't be afraid to try.*
"Spotlight"

I embarked on my freshman year with a stack of CDs
and a lack of confidence. When you're a teenager, feeling
misjudged and misguided and misunderstood comes with
the territory. You're supposed to strive for independence,
be your own person—as long as you do what everyone else
is doing, of course. I wanted to stand out and at the same
time, I wanted to stand on the sidelines. I figured things
would be easier if I just faded into the background. I would

<140>

still be an individual, I reasoned, just an invisible individual.

Thankfully, I had Madonna to serve as my tour guide through Teen Town, and she always steered me in the right direction. She was encouraging, persuasive, uncompromising. It helped that she practiced what she preached, that her messages were genuine, not gimmicky. Madonna would remind me, over and over, to express myself, even if I thought people wouldn't like who I was. She would prod me, relentlessly, to speak my mind, even if I thought people didn't want to hear what I had to say. Eventually, the words sunk in, and I realized that the perks of being a wallflower were few and far between.

Did I say something wrong? Oops. I didn't know I couldn't talk about sex. I must've been crazy.
"Human Nature"

It was a relief to find my voice, even though people gave me grief about it. Sometimes I talked about things that were too radical for them—what it feels like for a girl, for instance. High school is not a good time to be a girl. That's when people really start to make a stink about all that good girl/bad girl garbage. It's virgins versus vixens, saints versus sluts. Girls can't be prudish, but they can't be prurient, either. Basically, there's no medium, happy or otherwise. It's either one extreme or the other.

We girls go along with this because we think we have no choice. We don't want to make waves and rock the boat. We just want to fit in. So I let myself be lumped into the good girl category. It wasn't how I identified, necessarily; it was how others defined me. I wasn't rounding third base and sliding into home, I didn't have a reputation—well, not a disreputable one, anyway—and I felt like a virgin. So, yeah, I met all of the good girl criteria, but I didn't want any part of it. For me, the Madonna/whore divide was a totally different dichotomy.

Don't put me off, 'cause I'm on fire and I can't quench my desire.

Off the Rocks

<141>

"Burning Up"

Madonna is ad(wh)or(e)able. She portrays sexuality as fluid and flexible and fun. She champions female sexual autonomy, which, contrary to what I learned in high school, is not about using your looks to attract the attention of the opposite sex. It's about knowing your body and your needs and being willing and able to communicate those needs to others. Even if—more like especially if—you're a girl, you shouldn't be afraid to express yourself or explore yourself and, if you so desire, explore the selves of others. Besides, there's a difference between being sexual and being promiscuous, and if I wanted to have sex, if I did have sex, if I just thought about having sex, it didn't mean that I was a slut or a bad girl. It meant that I was human.

Shouldn't matter who you choose to love.
"In This Life"

Being human is like being in a variety show. Variety is the spice of life. Except when you're a teenager, and then variety is the vice of life. In high school, conformity is compulsory. So is heterosexuality. Girls are attracted only to guys and guys are attracted only to girls. Why's it so hard to accept that that's not always the case? As I learned early on in my idol worship, Madonna is a heroine to the queer community, and everyone knows that her fan base is comprised largely of, um, hag fags, if you will. Madonna has always advocated acceptance—accepting yourself for who you are and accepting others for who they are. So, when I realized halfway through high school that I batted for both teams, and that I might possibly prefer the girls' team to the boys' team, I didn't feel the need to deny or justify my love.

Tell me everything I'm not, but don't ever tell me to stop.
"Don't Tell Me"

<142>

I love Madonna. Not only because she helped me through high school, but because her influence has been so incessant. There's always something I can learn from her life or from her lyrics. I'm like her in some ways, but I'd like to be more like her, and I continue to aspire after the things that I admire about her. Madonna is a maverick. She has audacity, tenacity, veracity. She is gritty and witty, competent and confident, fearless and peerless. She may be my lucky star, but I'm the luckiest by far.

<143>

Aimee Herman

Ejaculating Beauty

"our bodies are beauty inducers" – j/j hastain

I practice being a girl.

I am six. I am seven.

A memory.

We play newlyweds before we understand the meaning of the word.

We dance around naked in my bedroom painted purple-scented childhood. There is no straight or gay or **love** besides what we see our parents making. There is just this.

We take off our clothes and our bodies look more like the floor we are dancing on than the clouds we name in the sky during the day. We are flat and unfinished. Lackluster and hairless.

At night, we speak through walkie-talkies. Her house is just a few away from mine, but right now, we are naked and we haven't learned the word airbrush or cosmetic enhancement or the formulaic entanglement of misinformed beauty manuals.

All we know is this music.

Tiffany screaming: **I think we're alone now. There doesn't seem to be anyone around. I think we're**

<144>

alone now. The beating of our hearts is the only sound.
We run around my bedroom, fluffing up our hair, throwing baby powder in the air like ghostly confetti, and then we stop.

Her vagina is a different shade of white now and I rub my fingers around, creating a chalk-like outline now found on New York City sidewalks.

I have no idea what I am doing.

Nothing. Much. Has. Changed.

I am seven. I am eight.

David Achbar sits behind me in first grade, where I find myself hypnotized by the fluffy hair and dark skin of Mrs. Schwartz.

He taps me on the shoulder and gestures for me to look down.

David's baby dick is dangling between his gangly legs, shorts pulled past knees.

I say nothing, though wonder how long I'll have to wait before what sits between **my** legs grows **long** like that.

My mother stuffs my torso in buttons and lace and I wonder if boy and girl gender can be interrupted by a third called **tablecloth**, called ironed out and lovely and fit for Thanksgiving china placed over belly and smooth legs and I can check the box labeled "L" for **linen** as gender.

"F" translated as folded and "M" for muddled and mussed.

Off the Rocks

<145>

In class, when we would line up in height order, then genital conformity, I would stand in my own line.

I was interwoven hair and blushed cheeks and scratched off scabs called scars on elbows and knees and pushed down breasts without the push.

Turn-ons included Super Soaker water guns banned by my mother. I'd sneak one from my neighbor, who fed my hunger for phallic shaped parts that could be strapped on and shoot liquid.

If only   I had known   then...

So, they called me a tomboy because the color pink made me squeal and dolls freaked me out and since when do colors and plastic parts assembled in China with blurred out privates symbolize disorder or mutiny of gender?

When I was 12, I wore grass stains on my knees, which competed with the elegance of hair braids and pink dyed fabric over elastic called scrunchies called girly called nightmare called   drag.

At school, I was the last one still appearing in undershirt beneath *over* shirt in the locker room at gym class. I'd stare at my feet as though they projected a **blockbuster movie** while girls removed their shirts, unclasped their bras with **one hand**, and allowed their newly gorged breasts to breathe.

They complained of period aches and bloatedness and broke down the discourse of tampons versus pads.

I knew nothing of this world and began to wonder if I could get a free pass into the boys' room. I looked more like them than these blondies in curling iron curls and shaved legs.

<146>

Shaved legs! At that time, I had nothing to shave off my legs other than my knees!

All around me, girls' bodies were swelling. I longed to be weighed down by hair and breasts and adrenaline for necking because I thought menstruation led to sex drive. Bloody uterine lining led to heterosexual exploration and if I could just start bleeding, I could *push* myself toward normalcy.

And yet, I also thought, if I don't start bleeding and my nipples remain lonely buttons like filled in potholes, instead of mountains, and my body grows hair but I permit it to remain rather than scratch it away with pink blades and if my vagina doesn't open up into this bloody force field, then maybe, maybe I'm not really meant to be *girl*.

My best friends called Marisa and Heather and Audra all had breasts puffed up like the third minute of microwave popcorn and they nicknamed *me* Mosquito Bites.

So, I thought maybe I could *itch* myself toward an intrusion of mammaries.

James Scarlucci throws a three-piece dissected bee at me in science class and calls me a screen door.

I become the one in charge of checking my friends for period stains on the back of their blue jeans.

I rub toilet tissue into balls, replacing the breasts that forget to grow on me, trying to appear convex.

My mother takes me to the mall, where big-boned woman wearing lipstick on teeth finds a training bra with built-in drill sergeant.

What happens in breast boot camp and what if I am just not ready to enlist?

<147>

My mother feeds me pills prescribed by doctors because suddenly my name or my predilection for *boy* things is alphabetically listed in diagnostic and statistical manual of mental diseases. Or *was* at some point and its ghost from 1968—the mention of sexual orientation disturbance—is loud enough to worry my mother.

And they ask me if someone touched me.

And they try and convince me that someone **must have**.

And I start to worry that they know something I don't.........

I yell:

I don't even know what I like yet

and I am not even sure what to think of this

and how can I be disturbed about something that makes me feel *me*?

So I practice harder because maybe this girl thing is like math, a formula I just need to figure out to fully compute.

What does **X** represent
so I can substitute it for the answer to the problem
of **me**?

I weave blond curls between scuffed-up fingers and practice knitting them into each other because girls wear braids not knots and I can *do* this.

I press knees together, not apart, when I wear pants-without-the-legs called skirt, called discomfort, called girl.

<148>

I grab lipstick from my older sister, who knew just the right way to fill in the lines of her mouth without dripping on her chin or getting on her teeth, and I used to use her brightest waxes as war paint, but I'm **girl** now, so I trace my lips and fill in the space and I smile and see teeth once white, look bloody.

What did I do wrong?

My mother buys me control-top pantyhose, and I am unsure of what I am controlling but somehow it is important to press **IT** down. I tell her the elastic and darkened stretch hurts my belly, which has no qualms about being flimsy or fatty.

Does being a girl equal control-topped body?

She fills our pantry with low-fat nourishment called Weight Watchers called eating disturbance called aspartame supplement.

My curves hadn't set in yet, but I was told to *watch it*.

Pay attention to serving sizes and count at least 20 times before swallowing.

Your metabolism is going to catch up with you, said my mother.

Suddenly, girly meant skinny.

When I was born, before they declared me girl with name ending in vowel, they pierced my ears to mutilate me toward my gender.

<149>

Girl babies just look so cute wearing little pearls in their ears, said my mother.

I dangled plastic from my ears and wore patent leather with raised heels on my feet over socks with twirls at the ends and a necklace against my collarbone, which felt like a boy or something in-between but looked like a girl.

When I was younger, I assumed I was born on a Friday.

Assumed the **F** meant Friday because that somehow made more sense than female.

What is in-between   **M** and **F**?

The slash.

The *or*.

Can someone just choose the slash?

And then,
I circle yes, instead of no, when boys ask me if I like-like them and would I be their girlfriend?

Boys whose voices were dropping and zippers were bulging.

Held hands with Daniels and Davids and Donnies and Damians and when kisses were requested, I let their tongues inside me because I was afraid of what it meant that I just wanted to say **no**.

At 13, I become a woman before I *officially* become a woman during a Jewish ceremony called Bat Mitzvah.

My parents had money back then and my dress was built out of hands we gave a check to and suddenly I felt like a

<150>

dinosaur, with back of ruffled scales and long, shimmering tail of taffeta, and a dinosaur costume would have been better than this.

I wore that dress. Skin shivered beneath iridescent hems and puff. My drag   queen debut.

Two years later, I get it. And my womanhood extends from Jewishness to uterus.

I thought I wanted it. Thought I wanted puffed up breasts like flesh-colored peacock feathers or those bubbles that arise on pizza slices that I loved to pop with my teeth.

But the moment I saw red, I cried. This is when the pushing began.

I tried to gather as much hair as I could over my vagina to hide it
because it suddenly looked beastly to me.

I am 14. I am 15.

I become a pro at sticking pads to my underwear and shaving my legs with battery-operated razor.

My parents send me to camp and I am placed in wood-paneled cabin with 12 other girls and at night, I sleep in top bunk of bed where below me sleeps a girl named Rebecca from Larchmont, New York.

I learn how to insert a tampon in my vagina by straddling toilet and pushing out/contracting myself.

We compare breasts and mine are the smallest.

<151>

I begin to covet their shape for the very first time when
Rebecca says, *If I close my eyes, I can pretend you're a boy
because you're still flat up there and you kind of smell like
one and...*

This is when I fall in love the first time.

And when Rebecca puts her pink tongue into my pink
mouth and she swirls her pink spit into my pink spit and
grabs my small waist with her pink fingers and presses her
pink bones into my pink bones, it no longer matters what I
call myself. It no longer matters what I got.

I am 16. I am 17.

Imagine me with blond hair all swirly and distracting like a
Picasso. My hair is what my sister used to reference as dirty
blond, an emphasis on dirty.

I trade in my dresses for jeans, torn at the knees from
running fast and falling without rhythm. My heels lose
their erection and my feet carry laces with rubber soles.

I walk home from school on a Saturday, jailed for six hours
for skipping class or walking out or speaking up; I can't
remember.

I walk upstairs to my room with purple painted walls and
posters and scissors.

My hair becomes the last part of me that is not mine
anymore. It is my mother's, who brushed it on days when
the knots screamed. It is my grandmother's, who always
begged me not to cut it. Asked me to weave it into her
white. It is—it *was*—my final attempt at girl.

With rust on the ends from the time I painted eyes on and
treated the scissors like a piranha swimming in the

<152>

bathroom sink, I gather them between my fingers and
begin to cut.

1. Inch for each twist of hair held by my mother,
who left me when I was 12 when I was thinking
about blood and my body and needed her to
translate this worry and needed her to tell me she'd
love me girl or boy or just the slash. Without
exchanging pills for potatoes as a side with my
supper. Without sending me into rooms to be
analyzed because I was lingering my looks at girls
instead of boys because being called a tomboy felt
more complimentary than pretty or girly because
we had good insurance back then and thank god
because I would need more than therapy to
fix/change/remove the   gay   inside of me.

2. Inches for my vagina. Feeling like I am
mourning something that has remained but become
something else. Has begun to stand for something
more than just a genital. Stand for something more
than the **F** after the slash following the **M**. A desire
to fight it out of me. Fight it off of me. Or somehow
change its purpose or clarification or justification or
intended architectural reasoning. And for the years
that will gather, where I treat my vagina like a
swinging door you find in restaurants separating
kitchen from dining room. Where I will not qualify
or question those who enter. Where I will not ask
about hand washing techniques or particular
preference for safe infiltrations. I will spend years
walking away from welcome mats, remove my
doorknob and doorbell and just wait to be removed.

3. Inches for my age and this year and this time of
my life, where controlled capsule without the easy-
to-swallow coating called high school called New
Jersey called 1996 force fed me media clips and
airbrushed air, which I had no choice but to ingest.
Where QSAs happened elsewhere, far enough that I

<153>

had no idea that it meant alliance. That it meant bridge of communication. That it meant help.

4. Inches for the boy in my high school that didn't make it. Decided to wrap his neck in knots made from Boy Scout training, rather than ask for hands to hold him. When he hung away his life, they finally started to pay attention. They wrapped ribbons around their brand new sports cars' antennas and missed football/cheerleading/math club practice to attend his funeral. And the boy who gathered his lunch quickly into his mouth each Monday through Friday in crowded cafeteria where tater tots and ignorance arrived on the side of each plastic sectioned tray. I always wanted to tell him to slow down. He rushed each bite as though preparing for war. As though bombs were just below him and he just wanted to digest before the eruption and removal of limbs.

And one more inch for that time the whispers grew louder and I heard the word **FAGGOT** for the first time in my suburbia. And the way this boy's face changed from careful to cautious to deeply concerned, in search of the nearest exit sign. The way they spoke it as though it was his name like Charles or Greg. *Hey, Faggot, did you get the notes from last class? Hey, Faggot, I'll bring my extra Nintendo controller when I come over to your house today.*

And for a small moment, I thought it *was* his name because he looked up at them. He looked up and just waited for what came next. As though what might follow faggot could be: *Hey, come sit at our table* OR *I'm not afraid of you or what I don't understand* OR *I'm one, too.*

In this inch, I cut away the shame. I take back words used as weaponry, but really just letters pressed together and I replace the bullets with blanks.

<154>

I am 18. I am 19.

There is a language for this part of me that could not be rubbed away, no matter how much I tried.

I learn a word that does not reach me until I am 19 because we did not have a gay club in my high school or in my town of suburban New Jersey or television programs with openly out, secure, and relatable gay characters.

Did I hear it in a scream? Pushed up against some kid against some wall between crashed fists?

QUEER!

Replacing tomboy. Substitution for the slash or maybe just another word for the slash.

Replacing length of hair or closet full of fashionable outcasts and inconsistent particles of cotton made in China.

Replacing my decision for what type of sex I liked.

If I was a bottom or top and how is that even relevant?

Replacing the history of a word. Or trying to.

Reclaiming seems too political. Instead, I patch this word onto a different pair of pants and suddenly everything looks so new.

There was no need to get rid of this.

This body.

This life which I spent years trying desperately to rub away.

<155>

Confusion. Convulsions of gender. The slash. The or.

Why is it we think:

We. Must. Get. Rid. Of. This?

I came out at a Chinese food restaurant in New Jersey on Route Nine, chewing on crispy noodles with my parents. Worrying about the language I should use to reveal that their youngest child was gay.

Called myself a lesbian.

Experimented with homo.

Dyke.

Butch felt fun.

Settled on queer.

Fell in love with spike-haired girls and mohawked girls and some with long hair in ponytails and pulled back by headbands dreaded into knots and shaved on the sides.

Moved in after the second month and learned the significance of U-Haul trucks and strap-ons.

When we broke up, I thought I'd never love again. Then it happened three more times.

Girls who looked like boys or used to be boys or used to fuck boys.

A mechanic with grease beneath her fingertips.

A hippie who loosened my heart like an over-the-counter diuretic.

<156>

The shifting of identities *within* my identity.

Wanting to hide my breasts, then pushing them up sometimes from carefully padded bras, then feeling uncomfortable by the stares and hiding them once again...the binding...the gathering...the shifting of and scratching away of...

Shaving off all the hair on my legs, then beneath my arms, and all those dark curls over my cunt. Looking like a little girl when I was old enough to drive, slurp alcohol, and vote for a man to declare war on our country. Thinking I was shaving it for *me*, but realizing it was for the girl with a pussy to match. She liked to find it easily, no digging through weeds before planting her lips in this garden. Hated finding my hairs between her crooked, dentist-deprived teeth.

Then, I meet a woman with a bush like a wild fern and I decide not to buy any more razors.

Suddenly, my cunt is hidden and I savor its secrecy. More to pull on now. More to play with. The encouragement of body hair yields a more prosperous imagination. Interference to elongate the learning process.

I pretend other things are hidden inside its tangled torso of zigzagged hairs. Pretend my clit is just a small dick that needs to be pulled on enough in order to grow more in size.

Until the interruptions. The questions. The glances and uncomfortable sighs from those who just don't **get** it.

Question:

So, do you want to be a boy? Then shouldn't you look more like one? And if you like pussy so much, why are you so obsessed with *dick*?

Answer:

I am thinking of a word for this. Or maybe I can congest it into a sound. Or a dance move. Or interlude of intricate gestures. Beyond gender. Beyond categorical configurations. Maybe I just don't want to be figured out.

On Monday, I stick my whole fist into my vagina and feel around for what may be hidden up there. I search for the **SLASH**.

On Tuesday, I dress my cunt up in streamers and lace like cotton-shaped birthday cake. My clit like a candle, I blow out several times until it's sore enough to grow lungs and demand a nap.

On Wednesday, I am boy or boy parts or masculine or **uncertain**.

On Thursday, I am **Monday**.

On Friday, I am **Wednesday**.

On Saturday and Sunday, I take turns, as the hours change, reveling in my inconsistencies.

My. Body. Weeps. Toward experimental beauty boosts.

Twenty-five dollars plus ten percent off for being the floor model elastomer cock climbed inside underwear beneath denim and pockets kissed against fur of cunt and hidden like a magical paper fortune inside an egg white almond folded cookie.

Press of various colored lipsticks over mouth, lasting only until mug of coffee parts lips or hands wipe paint away.

<158>

Mascara that is forgotten when same hands wipe away itch of eyes and lashes grow thin again...press of fabrics tighter to skin or farther away from...a tie or climb of masculinity over feminine appearing parts.

Fast forward through first Fridays when bars let the gays in to consume alcohol and consume each other and consume a night where hours feel purchased.

The realization of homos as consumers and rainbow flags marching with Coors Light flags, advertising what happens after gay pride parade marches on and the true digestion begins.

Sucking on cigarettes because tobacco companies *love* their minorities.

Sucking on drugs because we are still trying to *shush* away our executions.

I am 29. I am 30.

I gather the skin on my body like magical four leaf clovers found only from hours or weeks or decades of patient searching.

My closet is a schizophrenic approach to wardrobe.

I am mortar and pestle ground up nerves and identities and genders and sounds and needs and clarifications and blurs and words and poems.

I am queer, this word, this music, this distance between its beginnings—a past—to where it stands now—its present-led future.

I   understand   this.

<159>

Until.

Until you homos ignored me because I didn't look like you—not gay enough—dyke enough—femme enough—lesbian enough—political enough.

Well,

I got this lipstick

I got this hair gel

I got this mohawk

I got these piercings, tattoos

I got this strap-on, sex toy paperback manual for satisfying lesbian fucking

I got these tight pants, call them skinny, call them suffocation with a sales tax

I got this binding

I got this cock

I got this wallet attached to chain in back pocket

I got these chewed up fingernails

I got this leg hair, covering armpits and cunt

I got this membership card with no annual fee

I got this gay flag, rainbow recognition

I got this language

I got this body

<160>

I got this history

I got these splinters from **bursting** out of this closet

I got I got I got I got I got I got I got I got I got I got I got I got I got I got I got I got I got this.

What is left behind?

What is necessary to gather, stick in pockets, or throw away?

What can be   should be   needs to be   celebrated?

...the memorization of inconsistencies...to be both or three quarters of one and a sprinkling of the other...to be unafraid of asking what pronoun is most necessary...to understand the importance and need to ask...a widening of this spectrum...of queerness...of experimental language and representation...the poetics of homo...the song of body reclaiming itself...a celebration of contrast, incongruent gender, and unstuck designations through...

the ejaculation of queer   beauty.

About the Contributors

Adrian Ford is a longstanding member of NewTown Writers.

Aimee Herman is a performance poet. "Ejaculating Beauty" has been performed at NYC's Hot! Festival at Dixon Place and All Out Arts: Fresh Fruit Festival. Her full-length book of poetry, *to go without blinking*, was recently published by BlazeVOX (books). She can be found writing poems on her body in Brooklyn or at aimeeherman.wordpress.com.

A native of St. Paul, **Anders Krug Waalen** graduated in 2011 from Luther College in Decorah, Iowa, with a B.A. in Music Performance. He currently lives in Los Angeles, where he pursues writing, medical school, and singing countertenor. Anders is also a lover of mythology and a part-time manny.

Andrea Lambert is the author of *Jet Set Desolate* (Future Fiction London), *Lorazepam and the Valley of Skin / 730910-2155* (valeveil), and the chapbook *G(u)ilt*. She holds an MFA in Critical Studies from CalArts and co-curates the Featherless reading series. Her work has appeared in *The L.A. Telephone Book*, *3:AM Magazine*, *SUNSET.UNFO!*, *Chronometry*, *You've Probably Read This Before*, and *Tomorrow's Literature Today*. She has performed at West Hollywood Book Fair, Los Angeles Road Concerts, New Los Angeles Folk Festival, homo-centric, and REDCAT Lounge. Find her online at: andreaklambert.com.

Austin Eichelberger completed his M.A. in Fiction in 2009. Since then, he has taught literature, composition, and business writing at several universities, and in addition to teaching, he works at a rare and used bookstore. His work has previously appeared in *Eclectic Flash Magazine*, *Diverse Voices Quarterly*, *The Cup of Joe Flash Fiction Anthology*, and the University of Chester's *Flash Fiction Magazine*.

B.M. Spaethe is from Indianapolis and received her B.A. in English & Creative Writing from Purdue University. Currently an MFA candidate at CSU Fresno, she writes poetry that explores the LGBTQ community, urban landscapes, and human sexuality as it appears in the darker corners of some spaces. Spaethe currently works for *The Normal School: A Literary Magazine*,

The Levine Prize in Poetry, and in the First Year Writing Program at CSU Fresno.

Workshop director and secretary of NewTown Writers, **Barry Frauman** writes short poems and longer verse narratives: *West-East*, an American/Taiwanese gay male romance; *Gay Don Juan; Sons of New Town*, celebrating the Chicago neighborhood for which NewTown Writers is named; and *Crusades*, a volume of two verse narratives in medieval settings.

Caitlin Hoffman is a strange girl with a silly dream. She's written four novels, which she hopes to see in the bargain bin before she ditches this mortal plain. You can find her work in *Negative Suck, Arcane, Used Gravitrons*, and others. Follow her oddities @CHWrite on Twitter.

Chelsey Clammer received her M.A. in Women's Studies from Loyola University Chicago. She has been published in *THIS, Revolution House, Spittoon*, and *Make/shift*, among many others. She is currently working on a collection of essays about finding the concept of home in the body. You can read more about her here: www.chelseyclammer.wordpress.com.

Daniel W.K. Lee is a New York City-based writer whose poetry has been seen in various online and print publications. His culture and politics blog is: danielextra.net and he can be contacted at: strongplum@yahoo.com.

Dario Dalla Lasta received his B.A. and J.D. from Pepperdine University. A 2010 Lambda Literary Foundation Fellow, his erotic novel *The Three Red Lines* is included in the Lavender Library Archives & Cultural Exchange. His second novel, *The Force of Destiny*, will be published by Rebel Satori Press in 2012. http://dariodallalasta.com.

Denise Roma is a writer of short stories, poems, and essays. Her book, *Heaven within the World*, can be found on Amazon, and her essays have appeared in newspapers in California, Wisconsin, and Kansas. Denise lives in the Chicago area and shares a birthday with French poet Arthur Rimbaud, who turned "silences and nights into words."

Elizabeth Barrette writes fiction, nonfiction, poetry in speculative fiction, gender studies, and alternative spirituality.

<163>

She's on the Canon Board at *Torn World* and hosts a monthly Poetry Fishbowl on *The Wordsmith's Forge* (http://ysabetwordsmith.livejournal.com), writing poems based on audience prompts. She enjoys suspension-of-disbelief, bungee-jumping, and spelunking in other people's reality tunnels.

Gary McCann has been honored with two writing awards: the 2011 First Prize for Short Fiction from the Maryland Writers Association, and the 2010 Mystery/Thriller Prize, also from MWA. His stories appear in the *Harrington Gay Men's Fiction Quarterly*, Alyson's *Best Gay Love Stories, Mobius: A Journal of Social Change*, and *The Q Review*, in which "The Shape of the Earth" debuted in December of 2011.

H.L. Sudler was born in Philadelphia. He has served as publisher of *Café Magazine* and editor of the *Rehoboth Beach Gayzette*, as well as a contributing writer for numerous anthologies and publications. He lives in Washington, D.C., and is the author of *PATRIARCH: My Extraordinary Journey from Man to Gentleman*.

Ira Joel Haber was born and lives in Brooklyn. He is a sculptor, painter, book dealer, photographer, and teacher. His work has been seen in numerous group shows both in the U.S. and Europe, and he has had nine one-man shows, including several retrospectives of his sculpture. His work is in the collections of The Whitney Museum of American Art, New York University, The Guggenheim Museum, The Hirshhorn Museum, and The Albright-Knox Art Gallery. His paintings, drawings, and collages have been published in many online and print magazines, and over the years he has received three National Endowment for the Arts Fellowships and two Pollock-Krasner grants. In 2004 he received The Adolph Gottlieb Foundation grant and in 2010 he received a grant from Artists' Fellowship, Inc. Currently he teaches art at the United Federation of Teachers' Retiree Program in Brooklyn.

Jarrett Neal earned a B.A. in English from Northwestern University and an MFA in Writing from the School of the Art Institute of Chicago. A member of the 2010 Lambda Literary Foundation Writers' Retreat for Emerging LGBT Voices, his fiction, poetry, and essays have appeared in *The Q Review, Chelsea Station, Copperfield Review, Nolos, Lucid Moon*, and other publications. His essay, "Boys' Dolls," appears in the

<164>

anthology *For Colored Boys*, edited by Keith Boykin. He lives in Oak Park, Illinois.

Jason Orne is a queer Ph.D. Candidate in Sociology at the University of Wisconsin-Madison, a condition he should recover from nicely with time. He's been featured in the journal *Sexualities* and the magazine *The Morning News*. His next book is on Chicago's Boystown. He can be found at: JasonOrne.com.

Born and raised in The Bronx, **Martin Altman** graduated from Lehman College (CUNY) with a B.A. in English. He was featured at The Café and TallGrass Writers Guild. His poem "City Island" was published in *A Bird in the Hand* (2011, Outrider Press), and his poem "Advice to My Friend" is in the spring 2012 issue of *Obscura*, the Lehman literary magazine. His poem "The Reed" will be in *Deep Waters* (2012, Outrider Press). He has been nominated to "Best New Poets" (2012).

Marty McConnell lives in Chicago, where she runs the popular Vox Ferus writing workshop. She received her MFA from Sarah Lawrence College, and her work has recently appeared in *A Face to Meet the Faces: An Anthology of Contemporary Persona Poetry*, *Indiana Review*, *Crab Orchard*, and *Beloit Poetry Journal*.

Megan Backer-Bertsch is a queer poet and academic from Rochester, New York. Currently, she teaches English at SUNY College of Brockport and Finger Lakes Community College.

Nicole Goodwin is the recent recipient of City College's The Riggs Gold Medal Essay Award and was a finalist for the Brooklyn Film & Arts Brooklyn Non-Fiction Prize. She was also a fellow of the North Country Institute and Retreat for Writers of Color. A single mother, she earned her Bachelor of Arts in English and Anthropology from City College of New York in June of 2011.

O.C. Devanney is a terrible coward. She now lives a monogamous straight life in the suburbs and is using a pseudonym because she's scared shitless of the other soccer moms. She remembers her old lesbian life fondly, and one day, after her teenager leaves home, she's going to march in her hometown's Gay Pride Parade wearing a T-shirt which says: "Not as straight as you thought." Here's the good news—she can tell

<165>

you with authority that if you think that cute het accountant's wife is checking you out, it's not your imagination. She is. Because there's no harm in looking.

Robert Klein Engler lives in Des Plaines, Illinois, and sometimes New Orleans. Many of Robert's poems, stories, paintings, and photographs are set in the Crescent City. His long poem, *The Accomplishment of Metaphor and the Necessity of Suffering*, set partially in New Orleans, is published by Headwaters Press, Medusa, New York, 2004. He has received an Illinois Arts Council award for his "Three Poems for Kabbalah." View examples of his recent paintings and photographs on Facebook or visit him at: www.RobertKleinEngler.com.

Ryan M. Mattern is an M.A. student in the Creative Writing program at the University of California, Davis. He is the recipient of the Felix Valdez Award for Short Fiction. His work has appeared in *Burning Word, Criminal Class Review, The Toucan, This Paper City, Half Nelson, THE2NDHAND, Superstition Review*, and *Poetry Quarterly*. He is a founding member of PoetrIE, a reading series dedicated to showcasing the voices of California's Inland Empire.

Sarah Fonseca lives in a trailer in Lincolnton, Georgia, and an apartment in Savannah. Her work has appeared in *The Q Review, BtchFlcks, Autostraddle, The Lavender Review*, and *The Urban Resistance*.

Scott Wiggerman is the author of two books of poetry: *Presence*, which includes a poem first published in NewTown Writers' *SWELL*, and *Vegetables and Other Relationships*. Recent poems have appeared in *Switched-On Gutenberg, Assaracus, Naugatuck River Review, Contemporary Sonnet*, and *Hobble Creek Review*, which nominated his poem "The Egret Sonnet" for a Pushcart. A frequent workshop instructor, he is also an editor for Dos Gatos Press, publisher of the annual *Texas Poetry Calendar*, now in its 15th year, and the recent collection of poetry exercises, *Wingbeats*. His Web site is: http://swig.tripod.com.

Timothy David Rey is a Chicago-based writer/performer. As an undergraduate, he was awarded the Most Outstanding Author scholarship from Indiana University's Department of English, where he was fortunate enough to study with Pulitzer Prize

<166>

winning poet Yusef Komunyakaa. Timothy's poems, plays, and performance pieces have been seen and heard at venues throughout Chicago, as well as out of state. He is the co-creator of SOLO-HOMO, Chicago's annual queer performance showcase. Timothy has been interviewed on WBEZ (Chicago Public Radio) and in 2004 was one of the winners of Project Exploration, a writing competition from The Poetry Center of Chicago. Timothy has taught poetry and performance in Chicago schools, and his first chapbook of poetry and performance, *Little Victories*, was published in 2012 by NewTown Writers Press and is available at Lulu.com.

Tyler Gillespie's book of short stories, *Dirty Socks and Pine Needles*, was published by Sibling Rivalry Press in June 2012. He is currently an Assistant Editor at *Curbside Splendor*. He was born and raised in Florida, but now he lives in Chicago.

Vince Sgambati's writing has appeared in the anthology *Queer and Catholic* (Routledge), the *Journal of GLBT Family Studies*, and most recently in *Nimrod International Journal of Prose and Poetry*. His essays regarding LGBT parenting have appeared online and in print, including in *Lavender Magazine*, where he was a regular columnist. His short story, "Touching the Elephant," is scheduled to be published in *North American Review* and was a semifinalist in the *Nimrod* Literary Awards: the Katherine Anne Porter Prize for Fiction.

Walter Beck is from Avon, Indiana, and is a graduate of Indiana State University. His work has appeared in the *ISU Tonic, subTerranean 1 & 2, The Q Review, Burner, Off the Rocks* Volume 15, and others. His debut chapbook, *Life through Broken Pens*, has been released through Writing Knights Press to underground acclaim.

<167>

About the Editor

Allison Fradkin is one L of a girl. She holds a degree in Women's Studies from SUNY Purchase College and serves as Literary Coordinator of Pride Films & Plays' Women's Work, a writing contest for Sapphic plays and screenplays. Allison has a gay old time editing *Off the Rocks* every year. And when she is not on the write track, she performs in community theatre, teaches drama to people with intellectual disabilities, and goes rubber duck hunting. Her favorite sound is Fran Drescher's voice and her cocktail of choice is a Shirley Temple. She also has a fondness for Mad Libs, The Argyle Sweater, and The Baby-sitters Club.

9 781300 146599